Managing with Plans and Budgets in Health and Social Care

Post-qualifying Social Work Practice – titles in the series

Critical Thinking for Social Work	ISBN: 978 1 84445 049 X
Law and the Social Work Practitioner	ISBN: 978 1 84445 059 7
The Approved Social Worker's Guide to Mental Health Law	ISBN: 978 1 84445 062 6
Vulnerable Adults and Community Care	ISBN: 978 1 84445 061 9
The Approved Social Worker's Guide to Psychiatry and Medication	ISBN: 978 1 84445 089 3

To order, please contact our distributor: BEBC Distribution, Albion Close, Parkstone, Poole, BH12 3LL. Telephone: 0845 230 9000, email: **learningmatters@bebc.co.uk**.

You can also find more information on each of these titles and our other learning resources at **www.learningmatters.co.uk**.

Managing with Plans and Budgets in Health and Social Care

RICHARD FIELD

Series Editor: Keith Brown

First published in 2007 by Learning Matters Ltd.

© Richard Field

British Library Cataloguing in Publication Data
A CIP record for this book is available from the British Library.

ISBN: 978 1 84445 134 0

Cover and text design by Code 5 Design Associates Ltd
Project Management by Deer Park Productions, Tavistock
Typeset by Pantek Arts Ltd, Maidstone, Kent
Printed and bound in Great Britain by Bell & Bain Ltd, Glasgow

Learning Matters Ltd
33 Southernhay East
Exeter EX1 1NX
Tel: 01392 215560
info@learningmatters.co.uk
www.learningmatters.co.uk

Contents

About this text

This text is written primarily as a practitioner guide for managers engaged in planning and budgeting within health and social care organisations. The aim is to promote effective approaches to planning and budget management within organisations and prompt the development of associated competence.

Two main health and social care audiences are envisaged:

- students undertaking academic programmes that feature planning and budgeting;
- managers wishing to refresh, challenge and extend their practice.

In addition this text will also be of assistance to managers in other parts of the public and voluntary sectors.

Foreword from the Series Editor

Richard Field brings a rare insight to the reader in this text, that of an accountant who clearly understands the issues of Health and Social Care. It really helps to bring alive the debate and dilemmas of budgeting and business planning in these fields, issues that many in Health and Social Care wrestle with each day. The text therefore, written to support students studying Post Qualifying Leadership and Management Social Work Awards, is clearly of value to a wider audience. If you are a budget holder/manager in Health and Social Care or involved with business/service planning this text is a 'must read' for you.

Richard is a long-standing personal friend of mine and it has taken quite a lot of persuasion from me to get him to write this text, but I think you will agree it was worth it, and we still remain friends!

Another friend of ours, Ashley (a bank manager by profession) is always reminding us about his learning regarding targets – they always GO UP! The world of performance indicators and targets is now well established in Health and Social Care and frequently we forget to ask why we have Health and Social Care and what its purpose is, as we are so caught up with targets and performance indicators. This text will help you manage some of these tensions and help you deliver the best possible Health and Social Care service whilst understanding the broader issues of budgets, budget management and business planning.

I trust you find this a welcome addition to the Learning Matters Post Qualifying Social Work Series.

Keith Brown
Series Editor
Director of the Centre for Post Qualifying Social Work

Acknowledgements

The author would like to thank all those managers who have shared their stories about how planning and budget management actually occurs within their organisations. Particular thanks are due to those students who commented on an early draft of this text whilst completing the BA (Hons/Graduate Diploma) Leadership and Management Development in Health and Social Care at Bournemouth University.

This text will help the reader understand the following management standards adopted by the GSCC for the PQ Leadership and Management Award.

The agreed generic standards for leadership and management are those developed by the Management Standards Centre and published in May 2004. These have been adopted by Skills for Care and form an integral part of its leadership and management strategy. These management standards cover six functional areas and the text provides an insight into them:

- managing self and personal skills;
- providing direction;
- facilitating change;
- working with people;
- using resources; and
- achieving results;

This text also covers the following National Occupational Standards for social work:

Unit 15: Contribute to the management of resources and services;

Unit 16.1: Maintain accurate, complete accessible and up-to-date records and reports; and

Unit 17.2: Contribute to identifying and agreeing the goals, objectives and lifespan of the team, network or system.

Chapter 1
Introduction

This text focuses on:

- plans that are used for managerial rather than professional or personal purposes;

- planning processes and tools that can be used in many managerial situations;

- budget preparation and control as practised by managers rather than accountants.

The planning content is concerned primarily with business-level strategy within an organisation rather than corporate or operational strategy. Johnson *et al.* (2005) describe business-level strategy as being 'about how to compete successfully in particular markets – or how to provide best value services in the public services'. Likewise content relating to budget management is primarily aimed at cost centre rather than corporate management.

For planning and budgeting to be included in the same book is quite unusual as professionally, organisationally and academically these two processes are often separated. There is a growing recognition of the need for planning and budgeting to be integrated, the case for which is made later. For now it is sufficient to say that where this occurs managers will find it easier to engage in both processes and the outcome is likely to be more effective.

This book presents planning and budgeting in the order in which these should occur within organisations; that is planning first, from which budgeting should flow.

This book includes:

- written material intended to develop basic understanding of planning and budget management;

- activities designed to cause engagement with organisational practices related to planning and budget management;

- tips for success considered central to 'cracking' effective planning and budget management.

Chapter 2
Planning

Introduction

This chapter introduces planning from personal and organisational perspectives, identifies common variations in planning practice and explains how these are influenced by personality and context.

What is planning?

Planning can be defined as:

the process by which a desired future state is conceived and an effective way of delivering this developed and resourced.

This statement makes three important points.

- Planning concerns design, which should be a creative and hopefully enjoyable process.

- Planning is future based and should be aspirational, involving thinking beyond the current situation and any actual or perceived limitations.

- Planning involves identifying a way of making a desired future, reality.

Personal aspects of planning

All people plan. To completely avoid planning would require a person to act in an entirely spontaneous way, never thinking about what they might do next. Arguably even a decision not to plan is actually a form of planning – it is a decision about what to do or how to behave in the future.

During their life an individual working within health and social care engages in a variety of planning, for example:

- personal planning (e.g. career, lifestyle, pensions);

- care or treatment planning (e.g. care package and patient treatment);

- workload planning with regard to what they intend to do today, this month, this year;

- team planning with colleagues;

- planning for an establishment such as a doctor's practice or day centre;

- planning for a service such as chiropody or home care;

- planning for a major part of an organisation (e.g. a department, directorate, speciality);

- planning for an organisation (e.g. a voluntary organisation or hospital);

- planning with other agencies to commission or provide a service (e.g. youth offending);

- planning in respect of a project.

Whilst we all plan, the extent to which we do so and our approach are influenced by personality and context. As individuals we differ in terms of:

- the pleasure we derive from planning;

- the time we are prepared to devote to planning;

- how early or late we start to plan;

- the level of detail we include in our plans;

- the extent to which we engage others in planning;

- how easy we find it to depart from or change plans.

Comparing how two people prepare for a holiday illustrates this natural variation.

Person A starts planning their holiday six months ahead, booking flights and hotels, organising activities, making lists of what needs to be taken, using a spreadsheet to estimate and track costs. This person packs during the week before they go, ticking items off their list and double-checking their itinerary and timings before they fly.

Person B books their flights and hotel four weeks before their intended departure date, finds out what sort of activities are available but leaves booking these until they get to their destination. Packing is done the day before departure without a list and in the belief that anything forgotten can always be purchased on arrival.

Both holidaymakers engage in planning. Whilst the second person starts later and engages in less detail, planning has nonetheless occurred. Person B might actually prefer to 'take off' when they like but in practice will complete one or two actions in advance, perhaps as they:

- have young children that they do not wish to take out of school;

- wish to ensure their children are safe and secure and recognise that less planned or almost spontaneous holidays might involve 'roughing it';

- are in employment and need organisational approval for absence;

- do not wish to let colleagues down by disappearing at short notice.

How the two holidaymakers actually behave is likely to reflect their natural preferences as modified to fit the context.

One common difference between personal and organisational planning is that few of us in our private lives will prepare written plans. More usually the product of our planning is held in memory, captured on a calendar, or as a list of jobs to do, etc. Taking domestic decorating as an example, even those people who enjoy planning and know which rooms they intend to decorate next are unlikely to prepare a written three-year 'home decoration and renewals plan'.

Organisational aspects of planning

As with individuals, the amount of planning within an organisation and the way this is undertaken varies. All organisations engage in planning to some extent and in most instances this results in a plan document. In the private sector a significant driver for preparing plans is the need to secure loans and overdraft facilities. Similarly voluntary organisations require bank support but also need to influence or satisfy the interests of potential funders, so again are likely to prepare plans. By comparison, statutory-sector organisations are more likely to prepare plans because of a need to satisfy the requirements of the government and other agencies. In the current environment it is therefore virtually impossible to avoid preparing organisational plans.

Although the format of the plan may be externally imposed, there is normally freedom about the process by which this is prepared and the priority and resources given in support; this tending to reflect the personal preferences of powerful stakeholders.

Where organisational planning is less valued, the plan document may fulfil the requirements of external stakeholders but only limited use will be made of this within the organisation. Often there is a sense of 'going through the motions' with plan content based largely on what has happened before rather than on a considered analysis of what should happen in future. Documents prepared this way tend to lack vision, be operational in nature and lack linkage to the budget, a combination that leaves service managers vulnerable to 'across the board' budget cuts as they are unable to explain the importance of what they plan to do or how this links with the resources they claim to need.

Organisations that are led by planning enthusiasts are more likely to have a sound planning process and prepare plan documents that go beyond what is required by external agencies.

Planning can make a significant contribution to effective management, particularly where integrated with performance management, budgeting and other processes; these collectively ensuring that the plan is resourced, progress is monitored and prompt control action is taken.

Plans and budgets

Planning and budgeting naturally link, as shown in Figure 2.1 below, which assumes a three-year planning period. The plan incorporates a clear statement of purpose, measurable objectives and the key actions needed to achieve these. All activity, whether ongoing or new, requires physical resources such as staff time, buildings, equipment, medical supplies, etc., and the plan includes a summary of these expressed in quantity and quality terms. It is then a relatively simple process to convert this physical resource summary into a financial budget by multiplying the quantity of each resource required by the appropriate price.

Once the plan, which includes the budget, has been prepared, it should be subject to scrutiny leading to one of two decisions. Either the plan and budget should both be approved, or both should be rejected. As the budget is the financial expression of the money needed to acquire the physical resources required to deliver the plan, accepting the plan and rejecting the budget or vice versa is both illogical and unacceptable. Where the plan and budget are rejected, which is quite common, those planning have three main options; to change the:

- objectives which will ultimately affect the volume and/or type of resources required;

- actions by which objectives are intended to be achieved, this affecting the type, mix and/or volume of resources required and therefore the budget;

- physical resources that it is planned to use, for example skill mix, location, etc.

Figure 2.1 Integrating plans and budgets

Underpinning this approach is a belief that budgets can not be cut without planned activity being affected in some way. It follows that if organisational leaders wish to spend less money on a service they should recognise and take responsibility for the associated service consequence which might involve lower quantity and/or reduced quality.

If plans and budgets are linked, the manager will start the year with sufficient money to achieve the plan. If circumstances during the year differ from what was expected, resource consumption may be affected and managerial control action will be necessary.

Whilst the above approach is logical, plans and budgets in this sector are rarely fully integrated, especially at lower organisational levels. Over time senior managers, politicians and the public in general have become accustomed to demanding greater service quantity and quality whilst expecting budgets to remain static if not reduce year on year. Sadly the practice of applying budget cuts across the board is still popular with key stakeholders who appear reluctant to make or be associated with unpopular service decisions.

Tips for success
In order to be effective as a service manager you should:

- *Invest time and energy in understanding how much physical resource is needed to support your plan and be prepared to explain how this is calculated.*

- *At all times link your budget to your plan and refuse to accept changes made to one but not the other. This applies to plan/budget approval, explaining variations during the year, and reviewing year end performance.*

- *Remember it is impossible to cut a budget – but it is possible to choose to devote less resource to a policy, service, etc., providing the implications for service objectives and operation are accepted.*

Why plan?

If planning is undertaken with care and enthusiasm it should;

- stimulate service development by challenging thinking and current practice;

- ensure that services and activities continue to be relevant;

- lead to sustainable performance improvement;

- increase individual and collective knowledge of the environment, service users and service operation;

- provide early warning of possible opportunities and threats and offer decision-makers greater choice regarding the speed of any changes they deem necessary;

- improve risk management;

- build future capacity in respect of leaders, managers, professionals and other staff;

- lead to a shared sense of direction and a framework for decision-making;

- provide a basis for performance management;

- provide an opportunity to engage service users, staff and partner agencies;

- provide a sense of purpose and direction for staff, thereby improving morale;

- assist other managerial processes, for example budget management, facilities investment, staff development, etc;

- provide evidence of the service being 'fit for business' which is important to funders and other stakeholders.

The above benefits are impressive but will only materialise if the planning process is effective and well resourced.

Types of plan

All organisations prepare plans which vary in format, length and title, some of which are indicated in Figure 2.2.

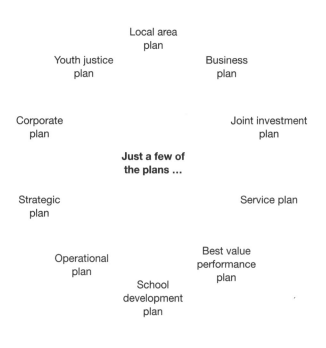

Figure 2.2 Types of plan

In the public sector different approaches to planning have been tried over the years, one notable example being business planning which emerged during the 1980s. Well known in the private sector, business planning proved to be rather alien to voluntary and public-sector managers. Part of a wider movement to adopt a business paradigm, business planning was initially considered relevant to parts of the public and voluntary sector that operate, or could operate, on business lines. In the 1980s and 1990s the use of business planning was seen in NHS trusts, services covered by compulsory competitive tendering and by some in-house social care providers in local authorities and charities. In practice, business planning proved difficult to adopt as:

- it required a significant shift in thinking by managers and politicians;

- some terminology and many of the associated techniques needed to be adjusted for successful use in a public-service context;

- the underpinning values can feel inappropriate in a health and social-care context.

This is not to say that business planning should not be used in health or social care; in certain circumstances it offers significant potential benefits, and many managers now use this in a modified form.

Plans can be categorised in a number of ways including these depicted in Figure 2.3:

Time frame	The period of time a plan relates to, this tending to fall into short term (typically one year), medium term (typically three to five years) and long term (normally in excess of five years).
Compulsory and optional	A number of plans are prepared to meet the requirements of external agencies or to demonstrate best practice. Other plans are prepared because managers within the organisation consider these to be of potential value.
Scope	Plans may be prepared at different organisational levels relating to a unit, a service or for the whole organisation. Often a hierarchy of plans can be found in an organisation.
Developmental or whole activity	Some plans focus only on those aspects of a service that need to be different in future and are developmental in nature. Other plans are whole in the sense that they address ongoing operation as well as new developments.
Fixed or rolling	Some plans are prepared for a fixed period of time, at the end of which either the activity will cease or a new plan will be prepared. Other plans 'roll on'; and each year a new plan is prepared for the full planning period. Taking a three-year rolling plan as an example, approval is specifically given for the first year's service activity and budget and outline approval is given for years two and three. During the later part of year one a new three-year plan will be developed and specific approval will again be sought for the first year this contains, which might or might not differ from the outline detail included as year two in the current plan.
Strategic and operational	Strategic plans tend to be informed by analysis and critical thinking regarding the purpose, objectives and actions needed for long-term success. Operational plans by contrast are concerned with the detail of how activities are going to be managed this year.

Figure 2.3 Plan characteristics

The following activity is intended to help develop your understanding of planning in your organisation.

ACTIVITY **2.1**

Plan characteristics

Identify the plan that is used to manage your service area and answer the following questions.

i) What time frame does it cover?

ii) Is the preparation of this plan compulsory?

  a) If the plan is compulsory, which agency requires its preparation?

ACTIVITY **2.1** *continued*

iii) What is the scope of this document?

iv) Is it a developmental or whole service plan?

v) Is it fixed or rolling?

vi) Is it strategic, operational or both?

Plan format

One of the key issues to address when planning to plan is the format to be used. For some managers there will be little choice as this is determined by external agencies or organisational leaders. Where this is not the case one of a number of possible plan formats can be adopted, each reflecting the preferences of those demanding or preparing plan documents. A decision is required therefore as to whether to use an existing format or design one specific to the context.

The format proposed in this book is based on three main sections: analysis, direction and action planning, depicted in Figure 2.4 as three triangles which combine to present planning proposals in a coherent and persuasive way. The purpose and content of each section is as follows:

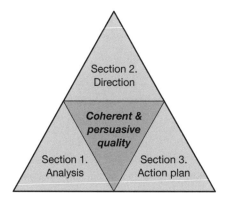

Figure 2.4 Planning to plan

Analysis section

The analysis section should help the reader develop a good understanding of the current and likely future context for the plan. The content should include a mixture of historical, current and forecast information regarding various aspects of the service; for example, changes in the environment, service user need, volumes of service commissioned or delivered, costs, performance, etc.

9

Direction section

The purpose of the direction section is to help the reader understand why the service exists, the key objectives and in broad terms how these will be achieved. The content of this section should be reasonably predictable by the reader as they already understand the current and future context for the service.

Action planning section

Once the reader has completed the action planning section they should be convinced that the actions proposed are realistic and, if the plan is approved, that they will happen. Typically this section will include information regarding what needs to be done, monitoring arrangements, resource estimates, risk assessments and links to other plans.

What constitutes a good quality plan?

Whether a plan is considered to be of good quality depends on the views of those receiving it. Typically evaluation criteria include the following:

i) The plan is informed by sufficient analysis. All plans should be based on an appropriate level of analysis either included in the main text, attached as an appendix or available as working papers.

ii) It contains actions aimed at achieving the best possible balance of outcomes for different stakeholders.

   Planning can be difficult in health and social care as different stakeholders may express different needs and wishes, some of which are likely to conflict.

iii) It balances short- and long-term outcomes. Often it is often possible to achieve short-term positive outcomes at the expense of future generations, for example by pushing financial and non-financial costs into future years. A good plan will however consider and balance short- and longer-term outcomes.

iv) It is persuasive. Plans are generally prepared in order to persuade others of the wisdom of proposed actions, to secure resources or perhaps permission to significantly change the service. Persuasiveness relies on the quality of the document, the desirability of the planned outcome and the impression given of the ability of those who will deliver the planned actions. A plan which may be excellent in terms of proposed actions may not secure approval because the reader is not persuaded of the wisdom of these or assured of the managerial ability of those who will deliver it.

v) It is useful. A good plan will be referred to frequently throughout the year and as a result will have a 'dog-eared' look to it.

In a well-managed organisation the criteria by which plans are evaluated will be known to those involved and developmental feedback given each time a plan is submitted for approval.

Figure 2.5 is an example plan evaluation form which includes criteria that explicitly or implicitly inform any judgement about plan quality. It should be noted that this example focuses on the quality of the plan rather than the merits of the proposed direction and action.

ACTIVITY **2.2**

Plan evaluation

Taking a recent plan prepared for your service or organisation, complete the evaluation form provided as Figure 2.5.

What overall verdict would you give?

Approval ☐

Approval subject to revision ☐

Approval subject to revision and resubmission ☐

Rejection, rewriting and resubmission ☐

Identify two aspects of the plan which you consider to be of very good quality or where further development is necessary.

1

2

Criteria	Explanation	Feedback comments	Development suggestions
1. Is the plan accessible?	*Is the plan written in a way that can be understood by the intended reader(s)?*		
2. Does the plan flow?	*Does the current situation and how this might develop appear to support what it is intended to do and is there detail regarding how this will happen?*		
3. Is the plan of appropriate length?	*Given service complexity and the needs of the reader, is the plan of appropriate length? If the plan is too short the reader may not have sufficient information for their purposes; too long and they may lose sight of the strategic direction or be put off reading it.*		
4. Does the plan contain sufficient detail regarding the internal and external context?	*Is there enough detail regarding the service context for the reader to understand whether the actions proposed in a plan are appropriate and feasible?*		
5. Does the plan appear to be the product of a sound process?	*Has sufficient opportunity and time been given for those with a stake in the service to contribute to the plan?*		
6. Does the plan show how this links to other plans?	*Is appropriate linkage made to other plans within or outside the organisation?*		
7. Is the plan self-critical?	*Have weaknesses been identified and evaluated?*		
8. Does the plan take account of the views of key stakeholders?	*Does the plan appear to be informed by stakeholders? Is there evidence of balancing conflicting priorities and long/short term perspectives?*		
9. Does the plan include a clear and justified statement of direction and SMART objectives?	*Does the plan include a broad aim or statement of purpose together with objectives or outcomes that together are Specific, Measurable, Achievable, Realistic and Time-related?*		
10. Is there evidence that planned performance is being stretched, yet realistic?	*Does it appear that assumptions about the design, delivery and management of the existing service have been challenged, performance levels checked against others and stretch improvements included?*		
11. Does the plan indicate the level of resources required to support the plan?	*As a minimum does the plan include a broad statement of required resources and budget? Does it appear as though more detailed analysis exists elsewhere?*		
12. Does the plan reassure the reader that planned actions will happen?	*Are the actions required to achieve the plan clear, responsibilities assigned and arrangements for monitoring appropriate?*		
13. Have risks been considered?	*Have risks been considered, are contingency plans in place and will key variables be monitored?*		

Figure 2.5 Plan evaluation form

Chapter 3
The planning process

Introduction

This chapter outlines a planning process and suggests a number of key questions to consider when preparing to plan.

Planning stages

The planning process that provides the underlying structure for this section comprises six stages, as depicted in Figure 3.1.

Figure 3.1 The planning

The first and often neglected stage of the process is planning to plan, where key questions regarding the whole process are addressed.

The second and most important stage involves three interlocking activities, which mirror the plan format introduced in Chapter 2: analysis, direction setting and action planning. This stage involves a mix of strategic and operational thinking which should be informed by various planning techniques.

The third stage concerns writing the plan document prior to presenting it for approval. It is important during this stage to allow sufficient time for plan contributors to comment on early drafts.

The fourth stage involves presentation, approval and feedback, as via an electronic or paper process.

The penultimate stage sees attention shift to implementation, which involves sustaining ongoing activity whilst engaging in service development.

The final stage of the process involves periodic reporting of progress against the plan, leading as necessary to management action.

Planning to plan questions

A poor-quality planning process can lead to excessive time spent on plan completion, disengaged stakeholders and ultimately a poor-quality plan document.

A good-quality plan is almost inevitably due to there being an effective planning process which can be shaped by answering the questions in Figure 3.2.

Key questions	Factors to consider
Who will receive the plan and for what purpose?	The answer to this question helps those writing the plan to tailor the content, style and tone to meet the needs of the reader(s). Where readership is diverse it might be desirable to prepare two or more versions of the plan.
What plan format will be used?	Does a particular format have to be used? If the format is not predetermined, is an existing one suitable or will a new format need to be designed?
Who should be involved in planning, and how?	Plan quality normally benefits from the involvement of a range of people; either as full members of a planning group, attendees at a planning event, as occasional contributors of ideas or draft readers. Different people have different perspectives and may well have information that will prove useful. However, the potential value of this involvement needs to be balanced against the time and cost involved.
What guidance and support will be given to those involved?	All those participating in planning will need to be briefed and for those new to the process it might be necessary to offer some training or other support.
What will be communicated to those not directly involved in planning?	Plan content is potentially of interest to all stakeholders and an early decision is needed about process and content confidentiality; options include total secrecy, regular controlled briefings or open proceedings.
What timetable will be adopted for planning?	The timetable for planning should be influenced by: • the answers to the above questions; • the final deadline for plan submission and any interim organisational deadlines; • peaks and troughs of work, holidays, etc. Planning needs to start earlier where more people are engaged in the process, where the linkage between plans is high or where funding implications need to feed into the planning and budget cycle of other agencies. However, the earlier the timetable starts, the greater the uncertainty about the future – more drafts of the plan will be needed.
What criteria will be used to evaluate the plan?	If the quality of the plan is to continuously improve, it should be evaluated each year. Those planning should self-assess both the quality of the process and the document, receiving developmental feedback from those responsible for plan approval.
How does the plan link with other systems?	Rarely can a plan be prepared in total isolation from other plans in the organisation and prior to planning it is worth identifying: • plans that drive or influence this plan; • plans that are driven or influenced by this plan; • plans that need to directly link with this plan.
Who will write the plan?	Whilst there is a tendency to assume that the most senior person involved should write the document, another member of the planning group might be more appropriate.
Who will present the plan?	If plans are to be presented at a meeting, consideration needs to be given as to whether this should be done by the most senior manager or the 'team'. Giving prominence to a team can demonstrate collective ownership and energy in support of the proposals and increase reader confidence. However, this outcome will depend on the ability a wider team has to present and deal with questions.

Figure 3.2 Planning to plan questions

Chapter 4
Using planning techniques

Introduction

This chapter describes a number of planning techniques that support the preparation of the three main sections of a plan. Also included are tips for success relating to the use of techniques.

A person who plans without analysis and strategic thought has little option but to base their decisions about the future on what has previously been done, what others are doing, intuition or whim.

A good-quality plan is the product of strategic thought which benefits from the conscious use of planning techniques, each of which offers a framework for gathering and arranging information or thoughts in a way that increases service understanding and leads to valuable insights.

In practice many plans appear to be informed by only two well-established techniques: an environmental scan and a strengths, weaknesses, opportunities and threats (SWOT) analysis. These techniques are quite sophisticated and various questions or checklists exist to support their use (Semple Piggot, 2000; Mintztberg *et al.*, 1998). However, whilst these techniques can yield valuable information there is a danger of overfamiliarity and lack of rigour. The outcome of a SWOT analysis in particular can prove superficial, possibly due to managers learning how to use this in contexts where a deeper analysis is not required or the common practice of presenting it as a neat four-cell grid, all on one page of flip chart.

Over the years a number of other techniques have become available to planners that can add considerable value to the planning process. These techniques vary in sophistication, the time required to use them and cost; some can be used in almost all contexts, others need to be used selectively and/or tweaked.

The techniques explained in this section tend to be relatively simple, cost-effective and generally applicable.

To gain maximum benefit from the use of planning techniques a number of factors should be considered, as captured in the following tips for success.

> ### *Tips for success*
> - When planning for the first time it is wise to select techniques that are relatively easy to apply and utilise existing information.
>
> - Gaps in existing information should be noted and rectified so that more sophisticated techniques can be used in future.
>
> - Always reflect on the experience of using techniques regarding the process and what has been learnt about the service, context, etc.
>
> - Try to experiment with one or two new techniques each year as this helps maintain the interest of those engaged in the planning process.

Completing the analysis

This section addresses seven questions, the answers to which will form the basis of the analysis section of a plan.

A1. What do we know about our performance?

A2. What do we know about how we operate?

A3. What do we know about the environment?

A4. What do we know about those that use our services and the services we provide or commission?

A5. What do we know about others that provide similar services?

A6. What do we know about opportunities and threats?

A7. What restraints affect our planning?

A1. What do we know about our performance?

The answer to this question helps the reader understand recent and current levels of achievement, should lead to successes being recognised and celebrated, stimulates organisational learning and provides information for assessing the feasibility of proposed actions.

There are three main ways of considering performance.

1. By comparing actual and planned performance, which results in understanding of the extent to which objectives have been met, or are being met. It also highlights part-achieved or wholly unachieved objectives which might need to be included in the plan now being prepared.

2. Comparing performance over the last few years, which helps those planning to see patterns and trends in key areas.

3. By comparison with similar services, organisations, etc., which provides a sense of relative performance and may indicate areas where there is scope for potential improvement.

Where there is a current approved plan this may include a mix of objectives that feature every year and others which are one-off in nature; for example, *to introduce a new accounting system by 1 April 20XX.* Performance in respect of both types of objectives should be reported in the plan.

Where an existing plan is available the following questions can help when reviewing performance.

i) What key objectives are included in the current plan? A key objective is one which if not achieved would have serious implications.

ii) What performance targets are included in the current plan?

iii) What is the current level of performance?

iv) Where current levels of performance differ from target, what are the main reasons?

v) How has actual performance changed over the last three years and why?

vi) How does performance compare with that of other organisations?

vii) Is there any additional evidence available to support claimed performance?

If this is the first time that a plan is being prepared questions i) and ii) should be replaced with the following.

i) *What aspects of performance do you currently measure and what targets apply?* These performance measures may be evident from organisational documents, inferred from the behaviours of leaders and other stakeholders, etc.

ii) *What do you consider to be important measures for your service and reasonable target performance levels?*

Figure 4.1 can be used to capture performance information. It should be noted that the first time a plan is prepared it is common for performance information to be missing – where this occurs this should be recognised in the strengths and weaknesses section of this plan and lead to action in the direction section. For some types of objectives it is not relevant to look at performance over time, or against other organisations so in these instances some of the columns will remain blank.

Depending on the circumstances described earlier, planned, target or reasonable levels of performance should be entered in column 2, current performance in column 3 and the difference between these in column 4. Where appropriate column 5 can be completed to show how performance is changing over time and column 6 where it is possible to compare performance with other organisations. The final column can be used to record sources of additional evidence or comment on the performance measure.

Objectives	Planned, target or reasonable level of performance	Actual current performance	Performance gap (column 2–3) and reasons	Over time is performance * Constant * Improving * Weakening?	Compared to other services/ organisations	Evidence of performance or comment
1	2	3	4	5	6	7
Reduce average gross hourly cost of home help/carer (PAF A0/B17)	£15.50	£15.80	30p per hour higher than planned	Improving given that last year this was £16.90	Relevant PAF average – £15.00	Although higher than planned and higher than the PAF average this is lower than last year
Staff opinion survey (Improved overall satisfaction levels)	85%	79%	6% lower than planned	Constant	Not applicable	A major reorganisation and irritation with the main computer system has impacted negatively
Introduce new management information system	£100,000 By 30/11/08	£105,400 By 01/02/09	£5,400 overspend 2 months late	Not applicable	Not applicable	Unforeseen problems with electrical supply
Achieve efficiency savings	2%	2.9%	0.9% better than planned	Improving	Not known	No comment

Figure 4.1 Performance analysis

A2. What do we know about how we operate?

Critical to maintaining or improving performance is understanding how different aspects of service operation affect current performance.

One technique for developing this understanding is a strengths and weaknesses analysis, the aim of which is to identify current:

● strengths that contribute to success and alert the reader to any action needed to pre-serve or enhance these;

● weaknesses that adversely affect performance and which if left unaddressed pose signif-icant future risks to the service.

It should be noted that strengths and weaknesses are often combined with external opportunities and threats to become a strengths, weaknesses, opportunities and threats (SWOT) analysis. Whilst many planners use SWOT there is a case for separating strengths and weaknesses from opportunities and threats. Separation often makes the analysis easier and tends to lead to deeper consideration and better understanding. The opportunities and threats analysis is often better completed later in the planning process when more is known about the environment, the market, alternative providers, etc.

Whilst a strengths and weaknesses analysis is relatively straightforward to complete, content relating to this in plans is often quite poor. Whilst sometimes this is due to presentation, more often it appears to be the result of failing to undertake the analysis in a sufficiently rigorous way, leading to plan content that:

- is simply a list of bullet points, the meaning of which may be unclear to the reader;

- includes strengths and weaknesses which appear irrelevant or of only minor importance;

- is generalised and of limited value, e.g. 'our staff' recorded as a strength implies that every one single member of staff is a strength and in every respect;

- includes asserted strengths which managers would like to believe but which are not necessarily true;

- contain little indication as to whether each strength or weakness is growing or reducing in significance;

- offers little indication as to whether claimed strengths and weaknesses are common to other providers of this service;

- includes only strengths and weaknesses generated by those planning rather than those that would be identified by other staff, managers, service users, etc.

In order to ensure maximum value is derived from the analysis a three stage process is suggested, as shown in Figure 4.2.

Step 1

Plan the process by which strengths and weaknesses are to be identified, analysed and assessed.

Step 2

Record strengths and weaknesses on a grid such as the one appearing as Figure 4.3, ensuring that:

- each strength or weakness is recorded in sufficient detail to make it specific;

- the impact of the strength or weakness on the service is clearly described;

- the significance of the impact of each strength and weakness is indicated using low, medium and high classifications;

- an indication is given of whether in respect of identified strengths and weaknesses this service or organisation is better or worse than others;

- an indication is given of whether the importance of each strength or weakness is decreasing, static or increasing;

- any evidence to support the claimed strength or weakness is stated.

Step 3

Decide which strengths or weaknesses should be included in the plan by selecting those that will be built on later. For example, if the plan records as a weakness *the quality of information regarding the future cost of care packages*, the reader will rightly expect to see an objective addressing this in the direction section. Whilst reported strengths may not demand any particular action, the reader should see how planned activities utilise these to achieve desired performance levels.

Figure 4.2 Strengths and weakness analysis – process

Strengths/ Weaknesses	How this impacts on the service	Significance (high, low, medium)	Is it a relative strength or weakness?	Increasing/ decreasing/ static?	Evidence
a	b	c	d	e	f
Strengths					
High percentage of staff with a managerial qualification.	Exceeds external expectations regarding qualifications levels. Likely positive effect on the quality of managers and therefore management which should positively impact on staff morale, care quality and performance.	Medium	Relative strength – a lot of similar organisations are struggling to meet even minimum levels	Static, having grown over the last three years	Quantitative information regarding numbers qualified. Positive inspection comments. However, no evidence that supports the link between qualifications and performance.
Weaknesses					
Computer equipment	Equipment is old, slow and crashes – service users do not get the service they should and staff time is wasted	High	Suspect other organisations have better equipment	Increasing problem	Staff and customer surveys have both cited computer systems as being poor

Figure 4.3 Strengths and weaknesses analysis – example

A3. What do we know about the environment?

This question prompts consideration about the environment within in which the service operates, how this might change in the future and the implications for the service.

The process by which this information is gathered, analysed and interpreted is known as environmental analysis, the intended outcome of which is not a precise prediction of the future, more a general sense of how the environment might develop, key themes and major challenges. Evidence of a good-quality environmental scan indicates that those planning are engaging externally and taking into account short- and long-term perspectives. The frameworks involved in environmental analysis help those planning to tackle its difficult nature, in particular the diversity of influence and interconnectedness, or complexity as identified by Johnson *et al*. (2005). The outcome of this analysis is likely to be a more strategic document than would otherwise be the case.

The literature regarding strategy and planning features a number of approaches to environmental scanning, central to which tend to be acronyms such as PEST and PESTLE. These acronyms provide a framework for the planner to identify environmental influences that are for example political, economic or sociological in nature.

The following approach to undertaking an environmental analysis recognises five major types of external influence: sociological, political, economic, legal and technological (SPELT). Irrespective of the period a plan addresses which varies according to context and preference, consideration of environmental factors should take into account three time frames: influences that are impacting now, those expected to impact within three years and those that might impact beyond three years, as indicated in Figure 4.4.

Environmental scanning involves four stages: influence identification, impact assessment, action and reporting.

Influence identification

The first stage is to identify key environmental influences that are affecting the service now or are likely to in future – these are likely to include some that affect:

- society in general as well as the service, for example increasing life expectancy and the implications this has for the level and length of care required;

- the health and social-care sector generally and which impact on the service, for example a shortage of nursing staff and the implications this will have for agency use, recruitment, employment practice, costs, etc.;

- the organisation specifically and which also impact on the service, for example a decision to build a new housing estate and the implications this has for service demand, capacity levels and service location.

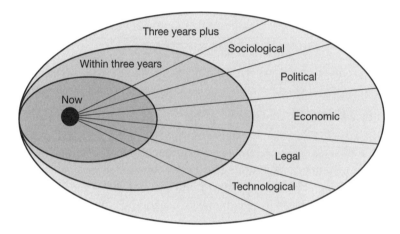

Figure 4.4 SPELT analysis

It should be noted that influences often relate to two or more categories. It does not matter which category an influence is recorded against; what is important is that it is captured and considered. The purpose of the five classifications is to prompt, not limit thinking.

Figure 4.5 indicates some significant environmental influences relating to a service specialising in treating liver disease.

Impact assessment

The second stage of the environmental scan is to assess each influence using the following questions.

i) In what way is this environmental influence likely to affect activities and/or operation?

ii) How significant will the impact of this influence be for the service?

iii) What is the probability that this degree of impact will be experienced?

Categories	Example environmental influences	Possible implications – (related to a liver unit)
Sociological	Population growth and composition, morbidity, mortality, lifestyle choices, trends in housing, care expectations, etc.	General increase in consumption of alcohol combined with changes in drinking patterns and habits. *High impact and high probability*
Political	Key policies at European, national, regional and local levels – changes In spending priorities, shifts in thinking about organisational forms and operation, etc.	Changes to paternity rights and entitlements *Low impact and high probability*
Economic	Key economic trends including employment, growth, inflation, interest rates, government spending, central and local taxation	Slowdown in UK economic growth, lower than anticipated tax yield – likely pressure on public spending *Moderate impact and high probability*
Legal	Legislation that is general, for example relating to employment and health and safety or specific to services, service users or organisations covered by the plan. Coverage would also include draft legislation	Changes in licensing laws allowing for longer opening hours – rising number of people with premature alcohol-related disease. *Moderate impact and high probability*
Technological	Includes developments in care practice and management, patient treatment, new ways of working, medical equipment, information systems, computer equipment, etc.	Potential advances in the treatment of liver conditions. *Moderate impact and medium probability*

Figure 4.5 SPELT influences – example

For many planners this assessment is reasonably straightforward, as can be seen in Figure 4.5. In more complex situations preparing an issues priority matrix such as that advocated by Luffman *et al.* (1987) can be helpful.

Action
Having identified the key influences the planner should take the following steps as appropriate.

1. Examine these influences in detail whilst this plan is being prepared.

2. Decide to investigate these influences in detail during the period covered by the plan.

3. Report in the plan that no immediate action is required but that the environmental influences will be monitored. This can be appropriate where the influence is not currently strong but could become so or because the impact is sufficiently in the future that action at this stage is considered unnecessary.

If either (2) or (3) is pursued this should be recorded in the direction part of the plan so that progress is monitored.

Reporting
To keep the length of the main body of the plan reasonable, detailed material resulting from the environmental analysis should be included as an appendix. The main text of the plan should simply include:

i) a general statement of how the future is seen, for example

The future is likely to see a continued increase in alcohol-related illness, a greater range of more technical and expensive medical treatments becoming available yet broadly static levels of resource

and

ii) any specific points you wish to draw to the attention of the reader, such as where you believe action is required, for example:

Of concern is the ever increasing difficulty of attracting staff given other health employment opportunities in the region and the relatively poor remuneration package.

A4. What do we know about those that use our services and the services we provide or commission?

As organisational plans significantly affect service users, consideration of their needs should influence service direction and therefore feature in plans. However, it is surprisingly common to come across plans that make little or no reference to service users, their needs or current levels of satisfaction.

It has long been recognised that understanding customers is vital to private-sector success and much has been written about the importance of retaining customers, encouraging repeat purchasing and attracting new customers. However, for many public and voluntary-sector organisations creating and maintaining demand is rarely a problem – on the contrary demand appears almost limitless as do customer or service-user expectations. The combination of limited resources and limitless demand exerts pressure on managers to increase service volume and drive down unit costs. However, this can compromise quality to the extent that the service has little or no value. Irrespective of volume achieved, if a service does not satisfy the needs of service users it is unlikely to represent value for money.

Irrespective of sector it is vital to understand and respond to service users, this involving:

- deciding which service users should be targeted to receive a service;

- identifying service-user needs for each target group and deciding which are to be met;

- designing and delivering services that address service-user needs at an acceptable cost.

Service users are rarely a homogenous group; in practice they comprise subgroups or segments each sufficiently different as to merit separate attention. In the not-for-profit sector a key decision regards which users should receive a service, or at least which sub-group(s) the service should primarily be aimed at. Where the service is aimed at more than one sub-group a further decision is required regarding the extent to which this should be tailored. Where service tailoring is successful levels of satisfaction should be higher than where a 'one size fits all' approach is adopted.

There is no universal way of grouping service users; this should depend on context. Common examples include grouping by age, gender and need. A profile needs to be developed for each group, this involving the gathering of information considered to be useful by those planning. Figure 4.6 indicates some of the information that can be useful.

Service user information	Group A	Group B	Group C	Total
Description and characteristics of each group	Under 11 Years	11–18	Adult	
Number of current service users	1097	562	3490	5149
Estimated number of future service users – next year	1200	650	3720	5570
Units of service currently consumed (hours)	32800	17890	65400	116090
Trends in service usage	Slow increase	Slow Increase	Slow reduction	
Pattern of use (e.g. frequency, length of use, timing, etc.)	etc	etc		
Identified needs	etc	etc		
Information regarding satisfaction levels	etc			
Expenditure by group	etc			
Income by group	etc			
Surplus/deficit				

Figure 4.6 Service user summary

Figure 4.6 is appropriate where there is one service and a number of subgroups. However, many situations involve multiple services and multiple user groups, in which case the analysis is more complex. In these situations either the grid above can be replicated for each service or a grid can be used which brings together services and groups in respect of a particular piece of information. An example of this latter grid is included as Figure 4.7, which shows where money is currently spent in terms of a portfolio of services and four user groups.

	Group A	Group B	Group C	Group D	Total of all groups
Service A	£1,000	£12,000	£0	£500	£13,500
Service B	£24,500	£32,000	£20,000	£60,000	£136,500
Service C	£0	£0	£0	£7,000	£7,000
Total service	£25,500	£44,000	£20,000	£67,500	£157,000

Figure 4.7 Service/user analysis grid

Gathering service-user information is challenging; however, the questions or insights this generates often prove valuable when looking at patterns of demand, resource allocation, etc. Figure 4.7 for example shows that:

- £136,500 of the budget (87%) is spent on service B;

- £67,500 of the budget (43%) is spent with service users in group D;

- service users in group D and receiving service B account for £60,000 of the total budget (38%).

In isolation this information is interesting but not necessarily useful. However, if this was combined with information regarding service-user activity it would be possible to identify unit costs, average spend per service user, etc.

This grid can incorporate historic/current information or be used to illustrate how the future might look taking account of anticipated changes in the environment identified using a SPELT analysis, as explained earlier.

Central to a well-developed understanding of service users is the extent to which their needs or wants are known. In this context a need is defined as being *something which is essential to a service user* whereas a want is a way of expressing *something a service user would like*.

Taking as an example a visit to the dentist, a patient might say they *want an injection* whereas they actually have a *need to avoid treatment pain*. Recognising the need rather than the want allows the dentist to consider other ways of minimising or avoiding treatment pain which might be in addition to or even instead of an injection.

These two concepts are often confused and those planning should focus on need rather than want. Identifying and responding to needs rather than wants is good practice as a service user may say they want something out of habit or because they simply can not imagine anything else being possible. How a 'want' is expressed may be quite different from the underlying need from which this flows and understanding the latter can significantly change service-provider thinking about clients and services. Failure to do this means that a need may remain unaddressed or under-addressed and satisfaction levels are lower than possible.

The importance of distinguishing between wants and needs is illustrated in Figure 4.8, which relates to a coach company offering a programme of days out for retired, relatively fit and reasonably wealthy people living in a particular town. The company has a clear target user group in terms of age, catchment area and disposable income; one which they have served for many years. It is easy for planners to assume that because service users continue to purchase a service they must be satisfied and therefore the future of the service is secure. However, continued use might simply be due to there being few alternatives or to users purchasing largely from habit. If at any point choice becomes available, personal habit interrupted, environmental change occurs or customer expectations alter the level of satisfaction and ultimately demand might suddenly fall. Those planning need to know how satisfied their customers are, the underlying reasons for this level of satisfaction and whether this is rising or falling. This knowledge will ultimately indicate the scope for increasing satisfaction levels through changing service design and/or operation.

Being aware that a need exists does not mean that a service provider has to address it; a decision often has to be made as to which needs a service will address and equally those it will not. Likewise a decision is often required regarding the extent to which an identified need is met.

Target group: Retired, relatively fit and reasonably wealthy customers

Service: Day trips

Expressed as wants	Felt needs
I want a nice seat with a headrest	I need to feel comfortable
I want to be dropped at the end of my road	I need to feel safe from personal attack when I get back home
I want a reasonable number and length of stops during a journey	I need to feel comfortable and relaxed about the length of time I will have to wait for the next stop
I don't want to be thrown about when we go round corners	I need to be safe and feel safe in the coach
I want to be able to get on and off the coach easily	I need to be able to do things for myself

Figure 4.8 Wants and needs

In this example many needs are present, the relative importance of which will vary from person to person. Each person identifies and prioritises needs differently and in effect has a personal balance of need for which they seek satisfaction. For the service provider different personal balances of need can be difficult to accommodate. In the example above, if the need to feel comfortable and safe is responded to it will probably increase costs and ultimately price – which some users will be prepared to pay. However, other users may be more interested in a low price even if a degree of comfort and felt safety are sacrificed. Where different balances of need exist, those planning could consider:

- focusing exclusively on a selected group(s), in the above example perhaps specialising in a rather more luxurious service where customers are dropped at the end of their road;

- compromising and accepting that some people from both groups are likely to be less than fully satisfied and may not repeat purchase; for some the service is a 'bit expensive' whilst for others it is a 'bit uncomfortable and uncaring';

- designing services that separately fulfil the needs of two or more subgroups.

Continuing with the coach example it would be quite easy to respond to a customer who wants to be dropped at the end of their road. However, this is simply how the customer articulates a deeper need 'to feel safe from personal attack when they get back home'. The company could decide to more fully address this need by dropping each customer at their door and ensuring they safely enter their house before driving off. Clearly there would be operational and cost implications associated with this level of service, which some customers would find acceptable, while others would not.

Knowledge of service-user need helps those planning to decide which needs to address, to generate ideas to meet these and understand the implications this has for service design and operation. Figure 4.9 develops the previous example by identifying for three user needs, some of the ingredients of service design and operation which the provider may flex in order to increase satisfaction.

Expressed wants	Felt needs	Provider ingredients
I want a nice seat with a headrest	I need to feel comfortable	Seat design, layout leg/head room, tray rests, individual lights, curtains, air flow, etc.
I want to be dropped at the end of my road	I need to feel safe from personal attack when I get back home	Drop-off arrangements
I want a reasonable number and length of stops during a journey	I need to feel comfortable and relaxed about the length of time I will have to wait for the next stop	Journey planning and publication of planned stops Clearly announced length of stops Headcounts before departure.
		Sufficient time to visit the toilet and have light refreshments, etc. On-board toilets, drinks, etc.

Figure 4.9 Wants, needs and ingredients

Identifying, selecting and meeting the needs of those users intended to receive a service is key to long-term profitability in the private sector and to best value elsewhere. This is achieved through

- avoiding offering service features that users do not need and may not even want, particularly where these incur cost to the provider;

- identifying important needs which if met would increase the value of the service at a rate that exceeds any additional cost involved;

- identifying and targeting resources to particular groups each with their own characteristic balance of needs.

Understanding the needs of service users enables the provider to target the most appropriate group(s), to be clear about the needs the service will meet and to organise and behave in a way that is likely to meet need and maximise user satisfaction.

Whilst poor service in the private sector may be punished with falling sales and reducing profit, elsewhere service users may continue consuming a service, particularly if it is free, simply because it is all that there is on offer.

A further characteristic of some not-for-profit sector organisations is that users are required to receive a service they do not want. However, even where choice regarding consumption has to be denied there will still be other user needs that a good service provider should seek to meet.

It should be noted that success involves more than meeting just service-user needs; frequently there are a range of other stakeholders each with their own needs, which may coincide, overlap or contradict those expressed by service users. A good plan will identify, balance and prioritise the needs of all stakeholders.

The final part of service-user analysis is to bring together the needs of the service user, assess the extent to which the current service meets these and identify the scope for better tailoring. Figure 4.10 shows how a simple service assessment grid can be used to capture this information, in this instance relating to a GP surgery.

Service user needs	How needs are addressed by the service	Current shortfalls	Improvement suggestions
To avoid sitting in the surgery for a long while when feeling ill	For emergency appointments patients are asked to join the end of the morning list	If there are a lot of emergency patients some will have to wait for more than an hour to see a doctor	Give emergency patients an approximate appointment time when they ring in
To know they can park their cars safely and not to have to drive round for ages before walking a long way to the surgery	A large car park at nearby shops	At busy times the shop car park is full and patients can not find a space	Little possibility of improvement in the short term – could make the use of public transport and taxis as easy as possible – leaflets, telephone numbers, etc.
To feel they are valued as a person	By the way in which receptionists, nurses and doctors talk to patients	No known shortfalls	None proposed
To feel relaxed in the waiting area	Provision of reading matter, comfortable chairs, clear signage, adequate PA system, etc.	Poor PA system – can be unclear as to which patient has been called	Upgrade PA system, invest in loop facility and improve signage to consulting rooms
To avoid having to take time off work to attend non-urgent appointments	Practice is currently open until 6.30 pm on weekday evenings	Patients who work away from home or in London have to take time off work to attend surgery	Open later one night a week and start a Saturday morning surgery

Figure 4.10 Service assessment grid

A5. What do we know about others that provide similar services?

Irrespective of sector, the planning process benefits from knowledge about how the service or organisation compares with other, similar ones.

Private-sector companies that provide similar services are usually to some degree in competition and planners need to understand as much as possible about competitors in order to find an 'edge'. For organisations operating without a profit motive the term 'alternative provider' rather than 'competitor' can feel more appropriate, although it should be noted that whilst not perhaps competing for customers they may be competing for league table position, funding, good quality staff, political support, etc.

The challenge here is to identify alternative providers that are similar, could be competing and are high-performing. The questions in Figure 4.11 provide a framework for starting to gather, sort and interpret information about an alternative provider.

Two problems exist; firstly, getting one or more suitable organisation to share information can be difficult due to confidentiality, time and cost concerns. The more competitive the relationship, the less likely it is that information sharing will be possible. Secondly, the quality of information can be variable. In practice those planning frequently have to rely on published sources or information gleaned at conferences, from contacts, etc.

Whilst alternative provider analysis might be difficult to undertake and there may be concerns regarding information reliability, this is still worthwhile. It should be noted that in the early years of planning, understanding about other providers is usually limited and rather anecdotal but this can be developed over time.

Aspect	Comment
What services do they offer?	This will help identify the range of services and the extent to which another organisation might be comparable
How large are they?	The volume of service, number of clients, financial turnover, full-time equivalent staff, etc., helps determine whether another organisation is comparable in terms of economies of scale
Who funds, or purchases, from them?	This helps to identify whether an alternative provider needs to 'win' money and if so, from where – this may help with assessing their level of vulnerability regarding sources of funding/income and deciding whether the organisation is likely to be competing
Where is their marketplace?	This should establish if an alternative provider is operating in the same market which might mean that they are competing for users, funders, etc.
Is anything known about their future intentions?	This might be gleaned from statements in the press regarding new services/new facilities and possible competitive activity, etc.
Why do those that use their service do so?	This might help with understanding what makes other organisations attractive to their service users – possible scope for replication
How financially healthy are they?	Using published accounts can help understanding regarding financial performance and how this compares
What do we know about them?	This concerns how the organisation is organised and operates; quality of buildings, staff numbers, pay and conditions, marketing, etc. This might yield ideas as to potential improvement areas

Figure 4.11 Alternative provider framework

Tips for success

- *When identifying services/organisations for comparison make sure these are similar to your own, and likely to be competing*

- *Select organisations that are similar to your own, focusing on those considered 'high' performers*

- *Assign responsibility for gathering published information about selected organisations to members of the management team*

- *Create a central reference point for storing alternative provider information as it is acquired*

- *Consider whether comparison should be taken a step further and benchmarking considered*

A6. What do we know about opportunities and threats?

Identifying, understanding and responding to opportunities and threats when planning is vital as this can prompt service development, growth and improvement in performance as well as protect against potential problems.

Four questions provide a framework for addressing opportunities and threats.

1. *What are the main opportunities and threats facing the service over the next few years?*

2. *What is the potential impact of each opportunity or threat?*

3. How significant is the likely impact of each opportunity or threat?

4. What is the likelihood that the potential impact will occur?

The starting point is to review the outcome of all the analysis to date and identify opportunities and threats considered significant. These might relate to a specific aspect of the earlier analysis, for example an environmental influence, or be the result of the interplay of different factors, for example an environmental influence combined with a change in identified service-user needs.

As this analysis can result in a long list of potential opportunities and threats, these should be assessed for significance and likelihood with the important ones included in the body of the plan. Figure 4.12 is a framework for considering opportunities and threats, in this example relating to budget pressure in a children's service.

Opportunity/threat	Potential impact	Potential significance (Score 1–10 where 10 is high)	Likelihood of occurrence (Score 1–10 where 10 is high)	Possible responses
1	2	3	4	5
Pressure on budgets relating to children and young people associated with an increased drive for efficiency in local government and media attention on older peoples' services	Children services are likely to be increasingly in the 'spotlight'. Pro-rata cuts, a rolling programme of reviews and increased member involvement are likely	7	8	Develop cost information Review high-cost service areas Undertake comparison with peer authorities Link plans and budgets Help portfolio members develop their understanding of the service

Figure 4.12 Opportunities and threats analysis

The proposed approach uses a scale of 1 to 10, where 1 is low and 10 is high, to explain the potential significance of the threat and the likelihood that it will occur.

The first column is used to describe the identified opportunities and threats, the second, the potential impact on the service. Columns 3 and 4 record the significance and likelihood scores. Where the opportunity or threat looks serious, column 5 should be completed, describing possible responses.

Without an opportunities and threats analysis planners might fail to receive early warning of a potential opportunity or threat, in the previous example becoming aware of a budget problem only when local politicians and/or strategic managers start to implement cuts, reviews, etc.

A7. What restraints affect our planning?

Most plans relate to part of an organisation rather than the whole, and those planning are rarely free to do what they wish, however compelling they may consider their case. Plans and the actions they contain usually have to be approved by senior managers, trustees and/or politicians, each of which will have their own view as to the purpose of the service and how it should operate.

A plan that fails to reflect the requirements and preferences of significant stakeholders is likely to be rejected. In effect a set of restraints exist which can affect many aspects of the service including target service users, purpose, organisational structure, operation, etc.

Identifying restraints, or 'givens' as they are sometimes referred to, can be difficult as these may not exist in writing and may be implicit, perhaps based on a particular incident in the past. As restraints are often deeply embedded they can seriously limit thinking, so it is vital that those planning know the restraints within which they are expected to operate, and are prepared to challenge these when necessary.

If the restraints are not clear, planners have three main choices:

- ask senior managers, politicians, trustees, etc., to clearly state the restraints that should be observed;
- state in the plan the restraints they believe exist so that those approving the document are aware that these have affected the proposed direction and planned actions;
- plan without regard to restraints but be prepared for the document to be rejected and the planning process extended.

If any identified restraints are considered inappropriate or unduly limiting those planning should consider:

- challenging the restraint during the planning process;
- making the recommendations they wish in the plan even where these run contrary to restraints;
- making the removal or lessening of a restraint an objective in the plan.

And by this point . . .

By the time those reading a plan have come to the end of the analysis section they should have a good understanding of the environment and service, unit, etc., and how this is expected to change over the period covered by the plan. A short summary of the analysis section can help ensure the reader understands what you want them to prior to considering the direction proposed for this service.

Setting direction

The second main section of a plan focuses on the direction of the service, the aim being to inform the reader as to why the service exists, what it is intended to achieve over the life of the plan and, in broad terms, the actions intended to bring this about.

This clarity is achieved by addressing three key questions.

D1. Why do we exist or act as we do?

D2. What do we want to achieve?

D3. How will we achieve what we want?

The terminology used to describe the why, what and how of direction varies according to organisational practice, personal preference and context, as indicated in Figure 4.13.

Section	Common terminology
Why	mission, aim, purpose, values, vision
What	objectives, outcomes, goals, targets
How	strategies, actions

Figure 4.13 Alternative expressions of direction

The content of the direction section should flow from the earlier analysis, contain no surprises for the reader or leave issues that have been raised earlier unaddressed. As an example, any weakness considered important enough to be reported in the analysis section of a plan should lead to action in the direction section.

D1. Why do we exist or act as we do?

This question is designed to elicit the purpose of the organisation, unit or service. Answering this question can be surprisingly difficult, particularly in respect of a long-established unit where the original reason for the service may have disappeared or those planning have never discussed purpose.

Many planners choose to answer this question with a succinct statement that captures the essence of the organisation or service. However, short statements can be bland and generalised, representing little more than a slogan. Other planners prefer more developed statements but have to be careful that these do not lack clarity and impact.

In practice there are some situations where a shorter statement is useful and others where a more developed one is needed. A logical response to this dual need is to write a longer statement that includes a succinct expression of purpose.

The length and style of purpose statement should take into account history, context, leadership style and how the statement is to be used. A matter-of-fact, realistic approach might be appreciated by some commercial stakeholders but is less likely to motivate staff. A deeper, more romantic style might inspire some staff whilst others may take great delight in pointing out instances where actions or behaviour are inconsistent with the statement.

Different forms of statement tend to start with a characteristic phrase; for example one regarding home care might start with:

The aim of the home care service is to...

Our mission is to be...

We have a vision for home care, for a service that...

We believe that those who use our home care service...

Figure 4.14 shows how, for a home care service, purpose might be stated using an 'aim' format.

We aim to provide a range of tailored services to users in a way that promotes their inde-pendence, secures an improved quality of life and helps them remain in their own homes.

Figure 4.14 Example purpose statement

The questions included in Figure 4.15 should be considered prior to preparing a statement of purpose.

Questions	Consideration
1. How is the statement to be used?	In addition to being part of the plan the statement might also be used for external communication, aligning staff to service aims, etc.
2. What format is to be used?	Will an aim, mission, vision or belief statement be used to express purpose?
3. What style of writing should be adopted?	Purpose statements can be written in a variety of styles including: • in a relatively factual and some would say cold way, as in *The purpose of the service is to...*; • more powerfully and with conviction, as in *Our mission is to eradicate* . . . ; • in a deeper, more personal way, as in *We believe in choice, in inclusion, in respect and all that we do we model these beliefs...*
4. How long do you want the statement to be?	The chosen length of statement should primarily reflect how it is to be used

Figure 4.15 Preparing a purpose statement – questions

The process by which a purpose statement will be prepared should be considered carefully and take into account available time and resources. A suggested process is included as Figure 4.16.

Drafting a 'good statement' requires those involved to be clear about what they do and don't stand for, value, provide, etc. As an ultimately convergent process this can be partic-ularly uncomfortable when the emerging direction differs from that preferred by one or more of those involved in planning. It is important to allow appropriate time for issues and concerns to be discussed, otherwise the resultant statement may not be owned at the highest level.

Stage	Comment
1 Deciding the purpose, format, style and length of desired statement	This stage involves addressing the key questions provided as Figure 4.15
2 Identification of themes, issues, ideas or words that should inform a purpose statement	In the earlier home care example (Figure 4.14) the key elements were: • tailored services; • promotes independence; • quality of life; • in their own homes. Each word or phrase suggests a value, a focus or a way of behaving considered important. As identifying, selecting and agreeing key terms can be quite difficult, sufficient time should be allowed for debate
3 Generation of alternative purpose statements	Generate a number of statements
4 Selection of preferred draft statements and review	Reduce the range and number of statements through general discussion and then review selected ones to ensure that • 'weak' words or phrases such as *like to*, *might* and *within the resources available* are replaced with more positive ones such as *we will*. Positively phrased statements are usually clearer, more motivational and communicate determination • each statement is consistent with the earlier analysis and that the purpose is appropriate, realistic and desirable
5 Initial testing, revision and selection of preferred statement(s)	Ask a small number of trusted colleagues to scrutinise the preferred statements and challenge the content, then revise as appropriate
6 Wider testing and final drafting	Subject the revised statements to scrutiny by a wider group of key stakeholders prior to final drafting and publication

Figure 4.16 Generating a purpose statement – process

D2. What do we want to achieve?

Having understood the broad purpose of an organisation, unit or service, the reader then needs to understand what those planning intend to achieve over the period covered by the plan.

The answer to the question 'What do we want to achieve?' should be in sufficient detail for the reader to feel able to start reaching a judgement regarding plan approval.

The 'what' of planning can be expressed in a number of ways; for example as objectives, goals, targets, measures, indicators and outcomes. Please note that for ease of presentation purposes 'objective' is used to describe how the 'what' of planning is expressed throughout this section.

Objectives tend to fall into two main types, those that:

• are likely to feature in successive plans, for example *keeping within the agreed budget*; and others that

• appear in a plan one year and then never again, for example *to reduce short term sickness to X days per person per year* or *to introduce a new human resource information system by...* Once a one-off objective has been realised it should disappear from future plans.

A good 'what' section helps the reader understand what it is intended to achieve, facilitates effective management and forms the basis of rigorous performance reporting.

Many plans include objectives that are of poor quality in that they fail to be specific, measurable, achievable, realistic and timed. An objective to 'reduce costs by 5%' might initially look clear and measurable but further examination raises a number of questions, including:

1. Which costs are to be reduced – is this all costs or some costs?

2. Is the reduction based on the amount spent last year, the current budget or some other basis?

3. Does this apply in year one of the plan, by the end of the plan or even each year of the plan?

A better expression of this objective is:

To reduce gross revenue spending by 5% in real terms year on year taking the xxxx/xx approved budget as the start point.

A suggested process for deriving objectives involves:

1. deciding how to express the 'what' of planning (as objectives, outcomes, goals, etc.);

2. identifying ongoing and important one-off objectives arising from the earlier analysis;

3. expressing the objectives in SMART terms (specific, measurable, achievable, realistic and time related);

4. testing the objectives to see they

   a) are of primary importance in that failing to achieve these would pose serious risk to clients, the viability of the service, etc.

   b) fit the organisational givens and are consistent with the purpose statement

   c) flow from the earlier analysis.

When stating the 'what' of planning a number of common traps need to be avoided, for example obscuring the strategic direction by including numerous operational objectives. Such traps can be avoided by observing the following tips for success.

Tips for success
1. Ensure stated objectives are

- *Clear and measurable so they can be translated into appropriate actions and then monitored*

- *Consistent with the purpose or the organisational givens*

- *Possible to achieve within the time frame and available resources*

- *Of primary importance*

- *Predictable by the reader in that they flow from the earlier analysis*

2. Where a number of detailed key performance indicators relate to a service these are often better grouped as one objective rather than individually

---

D3. How will we achieve what we want?

Although by this point the reader should understand the purpose of the service and the primary objectives, they will not how it is intended to achieve these or be reassured that these will actually happen.

Normally a considerable number of actions are necessary to maintain and develop a service over the life of a plan. In order to maintain the strategic focus it is important that the planner includes at this stage only those key actions required to achieve the objectives. More detailed actions will appear in the action planning section of the plan and still more in operational plans that flow from this one. This section should only capture the 'headline' actions intended to deliver the primary objectives.

A simple table such as provided as Figure 4.17 is all that is needed, this showing the high-level actions intended to achieve each objective.

Objectives	High-level actions
1. Reduce gross revenue spending by 5% in real terms year on year taking the xxxx/xx approved budget as the start point	Start a rolling programme of zero-based budgeting on 1 July 200X supported by an external facilitator
2. Complete a review of assessment procedures by 31 December 200X	Appoint a consultant with expertise in this area to undertake this review
3. Investigate and report on the use of hand-held recording devices by staff undertaking reviews by 28 February 200X	Commission a small team of staff led by an assistant director to undertake a study

Figure 4.17 High-level action summary

And by this point...

Having read the analysis and direction sections, the reader should now understand the context within which the plan is prepared and the intended direction. However, it is difficult at this point for the reader to be confident about approving the plan as they have a limited understanding of the actions envisaged, the resource implications and associated risk.

Action planning

The action planning section of the plan should persuade the reader that the planned actions have been thought through, are feasible, are likely to happen and will be successful.

The following questions are helpful in generating content for this section.

AP1. How will we ensure that the plan will happen?

AP2. What resources are needed to support the plan?

AP3. What risks are plan activities exposed to and how will these be managed?

AP1. How will we ensure that the plan will happen?

This question can be further broken down into three detailed questions:

● What actions are required to make the plan happen and when will these occur?

● Who is responsible for taking the required actions?

● How will these actions be monitored?

The answers to these questions can be presented using an action plan format as shown as Figure 4.18, which is a simple extension of the high-level action summary (Figure 4.17).

The action plan should contain sufficient detail of planned actions, timings, responsibility and monitoring arrangements for the reader to appreciate the potential impact on the service, staff in general and members of the management team in particular.

Completing the action plan involves the following.

● Inserting the objectives and high-level actions in columns 1 and 2 as already identified in the high-level action summary.

● Breaking high-level actions down into more detailed actions and inserting these in column 3.

● Entering key dates for each detailed action in column 4.

● Stating in column 5 the name of the person responsible for ensuring that each detailed action occurs. Usually this person will be a member of the management team although they may delegate this to a member of staff.

● Specifying the strategic monitoring arrangements, for example regular reporting to the management team, supervision, etc., in column 6.

A common problem with plans prepared at higher organisational level is that too much detail is provided. The action plan is not intended to provide the full detail of how objectives are to be pursued. This should be developed as appropriate in other plans such as the training plan, team plans, project plans, individual workload plans, etc.

AP2. What resources are needed to support the plan?

The resources needed to support the plan should be identified during the planning process and a decision made regarding how much detail is included in the plan document. This decision needs to take account of the context, how the plan is to be used and who will have access to it. If the document is for internal use only, inclusion of considerable resource detail, perhaps even the full budget, may be appropriate. With external readers, who may not need this level of resource detail, there are normally concerns about confidentiality. In many instances it is better for the plan to include only broad headline figures and for internal readers to be referred to the budget document for financial information.

Irrespective of where financial detail is included those preparing plans need to identify:

● the physical resources required to fulfil the plan; for example beds, staff, equipment;

- the money required to pay for the physical resources which will either be classified as day-to-day running expenses or one-off purchases;

- income from all sources.

This information forms the budget for year one and financial forecasts for years two and three of the plan period.

Objectives	High-level actions	Second-level actions	Second-level action – key dates	Responsible person	Monitoring arrangements
(1)	(2)	(3)	(4)	(5)	(6)
1. To reduce gross revenue spending by 5% in real terms year on year taking the xxxx/xx approved budget as the start point	Start a rolling programme of zero-based budgeting on 1 July 200X supported by an external facilitator	1. Appoint external facilitator 2. Brief staff 3. Develop programme 4. Start first review	By 30/04/0X By 31/05/0X By 31/05/0X Start 14/06/0X	Ian Charge	Include in monthly performance monitoring review process
2. Complete a review of assessment procedures by 31 December 200X	Appoint a consultant with expertise in this area to undertake this review	1. Prepare brief 2. Procure consultant	By 31/05/0X By 31/07/0X	Sue Preemo	Project management procedures
3. Investigate and report on the use of hand-held reporting devices by staff undertaking	Commission a small team of staff led by an assistant director to undertake a study	1. Prepare brief 2. Select staff	By 31/05/0X By 30/06/0X	John	

Figure 4.18 Action plan

AP3. What risks are plan activities exposed to and how will these be managed?

Assuming the organisation already has a robust approach to risk management and that this has appropriately informed the earlier analysis and direction sections of the document, all that remains is to identify and address new risks associated with the actions included in this plan. The aim here is to assure the reader that new or changed risks have been identified during planning, that these have been considered and will be managed appropriately.

The time spent on risk management and the amount of detail provided should reflect the size, complexity, and nature of the service, together with how this is developing. Specialist support may be needed where the level and type of risk are significant. For many plans, however, risk can be addressed by simply completing a grid similar to that included as Figure 4.19.

Columns 1, 2 and 3 should be used to identify the source of the risk, the nature of the risk and likely impact. Columns 4 and 5 should be used to indicate the potential impact and likelihood of occurrence by using a score of 1–10, where 1 is considered low and 10 high. Column 6 should show the impact of combining potential impact and likelihood scores to give a total risk score – the closer this figure is to 100, the more serious the perceived risk. The final column is used to indicate the intended approach to managing this risk.

Source of risk (e.g. primary objectives, environmental scan)	Description of risk	Description of likely impact	Impact severity (score 1–10, where 1 is low and 10 is high))	Likelihood (score 1–10, where 1 is low risk and 10 is high)	Risk score (Column 4 x Column 5)	Planned actions
(1) Objective. To reduce gross revenue spending by 5% in real terms year on year taking the 2007/08 approved budget as the start point	(2) Zero based reviews fall behind schedule due to poor management	(3) Budget will be overspent Unit costs may be higher than planned Service cuts may be imposed Adverse publicity Budget management may be taken back to centre	(4) 8	(5) 9	(6) 72	(7) Use organisational approved project planning methodology Monthly progress reviews with assistant director
	Failure to find 2% cost reduction	As above	6	9	54	Include external representation to challenge thinking Brief team thoroughly and undertake training needs analysis

Figure 4.19 Risk analysis

Summary

Once drafted the plan and the budget should be submitted together for discussion and negotiation, edited if required and approved. By the end of this process potential readers should have a document that is clear, useful and which contains sufficient information to address their particular needs. As this can be quite challenging, it is not unusual for planners to decide to prepare two or more versions of the plan containing different levels of detail, written for different audiences.

Chapter 5
Budgeting and financial management

Introduction

In a general sense everyone who works for an organisation has some responsibility for and involvement in financial management. The Chartered Institute of Public Finance and Accountancy (CIPFA), the accounting institute to which many public sector accountants belong, state in their good practice guide relating to financial regulations (CIPFA, 2001) that

> all members and staff have a general responsibility for taking reasonable action to provide for the security of assets under their control, and for ensuring that the use of these resources is legal, is properly authorised, provides value for money and achieves best value.

In addition, many employees are also directly involved in financial management, through being responsible for a budget, issuing purchase orders, passing invoices for payment, receiving and banking income, etc.

This chapter introduces financial management, which is part of the wider context within which budget management takes place.

Introduction to financial management

Although many textbooks use the term 'financial management', few authors offer a definition. The contents pages of finance books are evidence that this subject is broad, typically including:

- financial reporting;
- managing working capital, banking and investments;
- financial control, audit and risk;
- budget preparation;
- budgetary control;
- acquiring funding;
- cost accounting, short- and long-term decision-making;
- performance management;
- project and investment appraisal.

Financial management involves the intelligent use of financial tools and processes in support of the organisational vision. Service managers encounter financial tools and processes and therefore financial management, when:

- completing plans and exercising managerial control, including budgeting;

- reporting performance, including financial measures such as unit costs;

- making decisions, these incorporating cost and other financial information;

- assessing and managing risk to service users, staff, the organisation and society of loss or fraud, involving financial regulations and procedures;

- reviewing economy, efficiency and effectiveness.

Consistent with the breadth of financial management is a wide range of related competencies needed to run a successful organisation, as possessed by organisational staff and/or external advisors. In rare circumstances one person may possess all the required competencies but more typically and desirably, these responsibilities and competencies are dispersed throughout the organisation.

Sound financial management relies on a three-way partnership between accountants, administrative staff and managers; each with their own role, yet dependent on the others. Figure 5.1 summarises the typical contribution expected from each party, the overlaps indicating integrated working – in this example these could be developed further. In practice the size of each circle and the extent of overlap reflect the approach to financial management found in an organisation. Decentralised organisations have a relatively large managerial circle and smaller accountant circle, whilst the opposite is true where a centralised approach is favoured. Irrespective of the adopted approach, the extent of the administrator contribution and therefore the size of their circle tends to remain the same. However, where the administration actually takes place often reflects whether the approach is centralised or decentralised, tending to be at the centre for the former and within departments or service areas with the latter.

Arguably some aspects of financial management should be personally undertaken by managers whilst other aspects are better completed by accountants or administrators. Care needs to be taken to avoid duplication, gaps or an inappropriate sharing of duties, for example where accountants undertake aspects of budget management that should be part of the manager's role. An inappropriate sharing of duties can arise where a manager fails to engage in budget matters, where organisational leaders expect accountants to 'balance the books' and where accountants fear they will be held to account for overspends that lie outside of their control.

Managers need to be competent in those aspects of financial management they personally undertake, whilst in respect of those aspects undertaken by accountants, they merely need sufficient understanding to interpret the information they receive, contribute ideas and express views as required.

This text concerns just two of the above aspects of financial management: budget preparation and budgetary control, these being ones that managers tend to encounter early in their career.

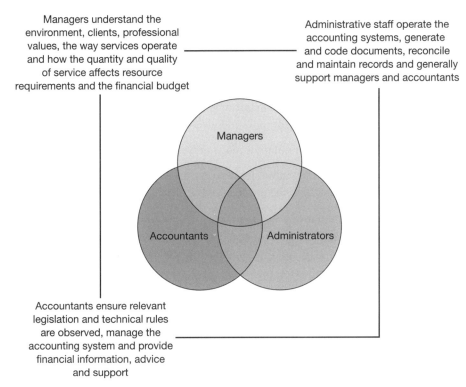

Managers understand the environment, clients, professional values, the way services operate and how the quantity and quality of service affects resource requirements and the financial budget

Administrative staff operate the accounting systems, generate and code documents, reconcile and maintain records and generally support managers and accountants

Accountants ensure relevant legislation and technical rules are observed, manage the accounting system and provide financial information, advice and support

Figure 5.1 Key player involvement

Although financial management should be an integral part of general management this is not always the case, particularly in the public sector. Failing to integrate often results in:

- plans that do not reconcile with budgets;
- judgements regarding performance being based largely on budget information;
- crucial strategic decisions made using incomplete or poor quality information.

Reasons for a lack of integration stem from:

- a tradition in this sector of failing to recognise the relationship of cost with activity;
- continued pressure to achieve high service volumes and efficiency often 'encouraged' by across-the-board cuts;
- insufficient engagement of managers in financial matters with a consequential over-reliance on accounting staff.

Importance of financial management

There is no 'magic formula' for ensuring effective financial management and organisational leaders have to choose whether to:

- make decisions regarding financial management as and when required;
- think strategically about financial management.

The former approach leads to dated, *ad hoc*, inconsistent and often contradictory approaches to financial management which in turn can lead to:

- low value for money due to poor resource allocation, monitoring and management;
- financial loss for service users and the organisation;
- relatively low protection for individual staff who may be exposed to false accusations of fraud or poor financial management;
- a lack of evidence that the organisation is managing resources in a safe and wise way;
- poor use of time with organisational leaders increasingly involved in financial troubleshooting rather than pursuing the purpose of the organisation;
- poor compliance with the principles of good governance and reduced public confidence and support for the organisation;
- finance being seen as technically difficult, shrouded in mystery and therefore better undertaken by finance staff – this leads to undue dependency on accountants and managers who become increasingly disengaged and disempowered;
- managerial 'game playing' focused on 'working the system' rather than the service.

Over time the decisions made regarding financial management form a framework within which the rest of the organisation operates. Whatever frameworks are set, managers can be relied upon to engage in practices that minimise any adverse effects for their cost centre. These practices, whilst entirely predictable and understandable, are often not in the best interests of other parts of the organisation, the organisation as a whole or even in the long-term interest of the manager concerned.

Practice regarding financial management is also affected by the quality of information systems and the behaviour of politicians, senior managers and finance staff. If information is of poor quality or behaviours inappropriate, these budget managers will in turn behave in predictable ways to protect or promote their service. Figure 5.2 provides three examples of poor frameworks and behaviours together with typical managerial responses.

It is not in the best interest of service users, the organisation or society for service managers to engage in game-playing and organisational leaders are responsible for developing an approach to financial management that minimises the likelihood of unhelpful or inappropriate managerial practices.

Poor frameworks, systems and behaviours	Typical managerial responses
Money that is unspent at the end of the year being taken away from the budget manager and future budgets reduced accordingly	Budget managers ensure they do not have unspent money by engaging in a 'spending spree' in March
Budgets that appear to be underspending during the year are 'raided' by line managers and the proceeds given to overspending managers	Budget managers will ensure spending is high early in the year, may overstate commitments, massage estimates of the year-end financial position, etc.
Draft budgets are cut by 5% to encourage economy and efficiency	Managers will ask for more budget than they need, knowing they will get less than they ask for

Figure 5.2 Typical responses to frameworks, systems and behaviours

To avoid the above and other unhelpful behaviours, leaders of organisations should devote attention to determining how financial management will occur in the future and ensuring that this is consistent with the overall recipe for organisational success.

Main elements and evolution

Effective financial management requires good frameworks, high-quality systems, competent staff and appropriate behaviour from all those involved, as shown in Figure 5.3.

The frameworks, systems, competent staff and behaviours of those involved in financial management need to be consistent with both the purpose and culture of the organisation. Furthermore, the overall approach to financial management needs to flex easily in response to environment changes.

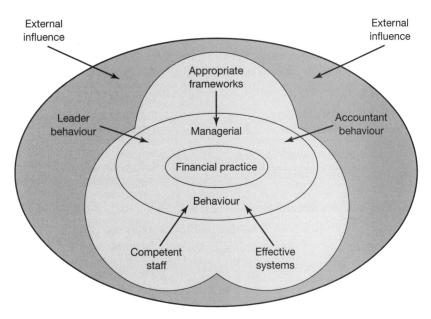

Figure 5.3 Financial management – overview

Frameworks

Whilst leaders of organisations may have significant freedom to determine the approach to financial management, they do need to recognise:

- external factors such as legislation, regulation, accounting convention and funding-agency requirements;
- internal factors including the values and preferences of politicians, senior officers and accountants.

In practice organisations use a number of frameworks to determine how managers will undertake budget management. The structure and scope of responsibility, roles and responsibilities, financial regulations and procedure notes, and plans, are examples of such frameworks, and are explored below.

Structure and scope of responsibility

Organisations tend to be divided into departments, services, establishments, etc., each of which is the responsibility of a manager who will plan and control activity. Typically these managers will also have a degree of financial responsibility, the nature of which can vary significantly within and between organisations. Information about costs will be recorded in a way that can be traced to these areas of responsibility, often referred to as cost centres, defined by Drury (1994) as being 'where managers are accountable for the expenses under their control'.

Organisational leaders have considerable freedom regarding the cost centre structure and the associated range of budgets. The scope of budget responsibility ranges from managing a limited number of budgets, typically those over which the manager can exercise some degree of control, to full budget responsibility where managers manage budgets that cover the cost of all the physical resources they use, irrespective of whether they can exercise direct control. Figure 5.4 illustrates both limited and full responsibility situations.

Ultimately the scope of budget responsibility is determined by politicians and senior managers who vary in their willingness to relinquish the associated power.

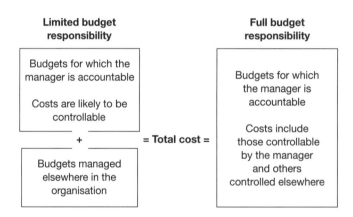

Figure 5.4 Extent of responsibility

ACTIVITY 5.1

The following table identifies four budgets relating to a residential home for older people – to what extent do you think the manager might be able to control expenditure?

Budget	Not able to control	Limited control	Good level of control	Full control
Rent				
Heat and light				
Food				
Equipment				

For many managers rent costs are totally outside their control, at least in the short term, whilst the level of control they have over other costs will depend on the framework within which they are required to manage. Taking equipment as an example, financial regulations might be set so as to allow full managerial control, partial managerial control or make this expenditure virtually uncontrollable by the budget manager.

Figure 5.5 illustrates how financial regulations might be set in a way that severely limits managerial control.

Manager can only purchase from nominated suppliers

Manager is not able to transfer money into the equipment budget to fund one-off larger purchases

Manager can only purchase approved items

Manager is unable to carry unspent money forward

Manager needs approval for purchases over a certain value

Figure 5.5 Control factors – equipment

ACTIVITY 5.2

Identify three budgets from within your cost centre and describe the extent to which these are controllable.

What changes would need to be made to financial regulations or other frameworks to increase your level of local control?

Managers of cost centres are usually required to meet a simple financial target – to keep within budget. Those with more extensive responsibility may find they are also required to achieve a target unit cost.

Whilst many social care and health managers are responsible for a cost centre, a few are actually responsible for a profit centre, defined by Drury (1994) as being 'where managers are accountable for sales revenue and expenses; for example a division of a company that is responsible for the selling and production of a product'. Whilst profit centres are more commonly found in the private sector this type of responsibility can be found in the public and voluntary sector; for example, where the public are charged a fee for a service or where one part an organisation 'sells' a service to other parts, e.g. a design and print unit.

Although referred to as a 'profit centre', in practice in the public and voluntary sectors the manager may only be required to balance income and expenditure or even to keep within a target loss figure. The definition of what constitutes a profit centre does not therefore depend on the intended or actual financial outcome nor is it simply to do with having responsibility for income; indeed many cost centres have minor sources of income, for example from charging staff for making private telephone calls.

Profit centres tend to share a number of characteristics including that:

- income is usually a significant element in financing the service;
- income is not guaranteed or predictable and has to be 'earned' from customers, pur-chasers or grant-givers;
- a failure to generate budgeted income might well lead to the cessation of the profit centre;
- the manager tends to worry about the volume of work and price they charge as much, if not more than they do about the level of expenditure;
- business planning rather than service planning is appropriate;
- the manager might be allowed to carry any surplus funds over at the end of the year or set a deficit against earlier surpluses – this depends on the financial regulations of the organisation and does not automatically apply;
- performance reporting tends to be similar to that found in the private sector;
- overall 'bottom line' financial targets are likely to be set in terms of surplus, deficit or break-even.

Roles and responsibilities

A clear allocation of financial roles and responsibilities is crucial to effective financial man-agement. These roles include budget management, income collection and recovery, petty cash management, order processing, inventory management, stock control, etc.

Financial responsibilities should be included in job descriptions and the organisation should maintain a register that shows for each budget the name of the manager responsi-ble. Each budget manager should:

- be aware of the financial responsibilities related to their job;
- understand how their financial performance will be measured;
- know the regulations relevant to their responsibilities;
- possess the competencies associated with the effective discharge of their role.

Financial regulations and procedure notes

Financial regulations specify what managers must and must not do and procedure notes set out how to comply with these regulations in a consistent, efficient and effective way.

Financial regulations and procedure notes form a vital part of internal control and compli-ance with these should be routinely checked to reduce the risk of financial loss, fraud, inefficiency and harm to staff.

ACTIVITY **5.3**

Find the financial regulations of your organisation and any associated procedure notes.*

By reference to your job description and current work responsibilities read those parts of the financial regulations and associated procedures that apply to you.

Note below any areas that you are not clear about, ask the relevant person for clarification and record the outcome.

Areas of clarification	Outcome

* Whilst most organisations have financial regulations or the equivalent, fewer have written procedure notes at least within a single definitive document.

Plans

Financial management should be an integral part of service management. As explored earlier, plans are the means by which direction and intent are described and the budget is simply the financial expression of the cost of acquiring the use of the physical resources needed to provide the planned service or activity. The plan therefore becomes a vital framework for budget management in particular and financial management in general.

Unfortunately in practice plans and budgets are often poorly linked, which makes performance management difficult and leaves the manager particularly vulnerable to pressure to:

- cut planned expenditure whilst maintaining service volume and quality;
- increase service volume and/or quality but within existing budget levels;
- cut expenditure levels whilst increasing service volume and/or quality.

Repeated yielding to any of these pressures should be impossible otherwise ultimately the result will be a service that provides infinite volume at maximum quality, but which requires no resources – a neat trick. Even if in early years of financial constraint some savings may be possible without adversely affecting the service, a point will be reached after which further savings can only be achieved by:

- reducing service quality, probably initially in areas not reflected in service standards or performance indicators;

- staff 'volunteering' to work in excess of contract hours without pay, in effect offering a hidden personal subsidy arising from a personal commitment to service users, fears regarding job security, or in the mistaken belief that this is only a short-term necessity;

- passing expenses to the next generation of taxpayers, for example by allowing buildings, equipment and other resources to quietly deteriorate.

If this pressure is replaced by plan and budget integration then a reduction in allocated resources is balanced by a reduction in the quantity and/or quality of planned activity – an honest and transparent approach.

Effective systems

Effective financial management requires good-quality financial and service information.

The principal source of financial information is usually the main accounting system, as operated by finance staff, and which processes vast quantities of transactions each year. However sophisticated this system may be it is unlikely to satisfy all the financial information needs of managers who therefore inevitably maintain some local systems, for example in respect of official orders placed for which invoices have not been paid, grant claims, bid information, unit cost data, etc.

Increasingly public service managers are asked for information that requires finance and service data to be combined, as for example with unit costs. This is quite a challenge, particularly as separate systems still exist in many organisations.

High-quality financial information requires well designed and correctly operated systems. Regulations, procedure notes and compliance monitoring help ensure that these remain effective.

ACTIVITY **5.4**

What arrangements exist within your service for checking that staff comply with financial regulations?

Competent staff

Successful financial management requires that everyone involved is competent, which in turn necessitates the regular review and addressing of individual development needs associated with financial frameworks, systems, processes and financial techniques.

Unfortunately, expenditure on developing financial competence is often allocated to meeting the needs of managers and accountants rather than administrators. The lack of training for administrative staff can lead to inconsistent practice across an organisation and with accountant development tending to focus on updating technical knowledge it is only managers that are likely to consider financial management as it relates to their service.

Financial management is far from just a collection of processes or techniques. Success depends on accountants, administrators and managers understanding and valuing each other and being able to collaborate to provide good-quality financial and management information.

Chapter 6
The budget manager role

Introduction

The following material examines the role of budget manager by reference to the degree of decentralisation within the organisation and whether budgets are devolved or delegated. The nature of responsibilities and rights is also explored, as are the associated financial competences.

Decentralisation, devolution and delegation

Whilst the budgets of a very small organisation may be managed effectively by one person, this approach is not normally possible or appropriate for larger and more complex organisations; a degree of decentralisation is usually required, this defined by Bean and Hussey (1996) as being:

> Where the control of budgets is disaggregated from the centre and allocated to other areas of the organisation such as departments, divisions, branches, etc.

Organisational leaders determine both the extent of decentralisation within the organisation and the nature of managerial responsibility, this normally being either devolved or delegated in nature.

Devolved budget management is defined by Bean and Hussey (1996) as being:

> The process whereby budgets are devolved to an individual who becomes the budget holder and who will be totally responsible and accountable for that budget. Ideally management and financial responsibilities are aligned such that the budget holder is accountable for the financial implications of his/her management decisions.

The term 'totally responsible' is important and needs qualification. The devolved budget holder is responsible for taking any action that is within their authority, otherwise they have a responsibility for escalating the situation by alerting their line manager as soon as possible.

The delegated approach is defined by Bean and Hussey (1996) as being:

> Where budgets are delegated to nominated budget holders who are responsible for monitoring the budget, but are not accountable for the budget as they will have little or no control over its construction and its usage.

By comparison with devolved budgeting, delegated responsibility is limited with the budget holder simply required to:

- spend an allocated budget on agreed types of purchase, broadly in line with an anticipated pattern of expenditure throughout the year;

- regularly monitor the budget, investigate and report problems to the person who actually holds devolved responsibility.

In larger organisations there may be considerable decentralisation of budgets, some of which are devolved, others delegated.

Although both the devolved and delegated approaches are valid and can be effective, in recent years devolution has become more fashionable. However, it is quite common to find organisations that claim to have devolved budgets when the practice is really a confused and ineffective combination of devolution and delegation, a form of pseudo-devolution.

Figure 6.1 summarises the main differences between devolved and delegated approaches and compares these with pseudo-devolved.

For the devolved budget manager the budget represents a financial target which, as with other targets, they should understand and believe to be fair, yet challenging. A reasonable expectation therefore is that a devolved budget manager will have adequate opportunities to be involved in budget preparation, negotiation and control.

Having a reasonable degree of freedom to act, which might include for example the ability to move money from one budget to another or choice as to where purchases can be made, is also important to managers with devolved responsibility.

Involvement in budget preparation and negotiation is much less important to the delegated budget manager. As their responsibility is less onerous it is acceptable for a delegated budget manager to be given a budget together with guidance regarding the purpose for which this is to be used. The main task of the delegated budget holder is to periodically examine the budget position, investigate problems as they arise and alert their line manager to under- or overspends that exceed a predetermined amount. Subsequent action in response to the budget position rests with the manager who has delegated this responsibility.

Limited freedom to act is appropriate to delegated responsibility as in effect the manager is only administering the budget.

With pseudo-devolution the manager is made to feel fully responsible for achieving the budget whilst denied involvement in preparation. The manager is left unaware of the assumptions underlying the budget and suspicious that it may be insufficient to resource the plan. This problem is compounded where the budget manager has little freedom to react to emerging budget underspends or overspends. Whereas budget devolution causes power to shift down the organisation, with pseudo-devolution, it is stress rather than power that is devolved.

Type of responsibility …	Clear delegated	Clear devolved	Pseudo-devolved
Extent of responsibility …	Limited	Full	Felt full
Managerial involvement in the process …	Receive budget Understand it Monitor it	Prepare budget Negotiate it Control it	Low or no managerial involvement in budget preparation Cope with it
Framework of rules …	Little freedom (appropriate)	Lot of freedom (appropriate)	Little freedom (inappropriate)
Outcome …	Administration	Management	Pseudo-management

Figure 6.1 Approaches to budget management

Financial responsibilities

For many managers budget management is their main but not necessarily only financial responsibility. Managers in different service areas and at different managerial levels may have quite varied financial responsibilities, the full extent of which should be clear from their job description.

Effective budget management is dependent on politicians, leaders and accountants acknowledging and responding to the rights of the budget manager, the number and nature of which vary according to whether responsibility is devolved or delegated.

Figure 6.2 suggests some of the responsibilities and rights relevant to a devolved budget manager operating at a relatively low organisational level. It should be noted that the 'rights' associated with budget management are not widely recognised, at least formally, within organisations.

The approach to financial management should be regularly reviewed to ensure it supports the intended culture of the organisation. This review should also consider the responsibilities and rights of budget managers.

Financial responsibilities Your are responsible for	Financial rights You have the right to
• Reading and ensuring you understand and keep up to date with financial regulations and procedures	• Know if you are a budget holder and to be aware of the quantity and quality of service to be achieved with the approved budget
• Participating fully in budget preparation	• Know the nature of your financial responsibility and the performance target(s) that apply.
• Undertaking monthly budget monitoring and year-end projecting, taking action as required to keep within the approved budget	• Be properly involved in preparing, negotiating and agreeing a challenging yet achievable budget
• Alerting senior managers and finance staff at the earliest opportunity to actual or projected budget under/overspends, fraud, etc.	• Know the amount of your budget before the financial year starts
• Ensuring that relevant information informs plans, funding bids, performance management and decisions	• Be consulted before any changes are made to the agreed budget during the year
• Discharging other financial duties in a timely and professional manner, e.g. grant claims, invoice raising	• Receive advance notice of planned charges to your cost centre and have the opportunity to check, challenge and agree to these
• Monitoring observance of financial regulations and process	• Be informed of the financial regulations and procedures within which you are required to work
• Pursuing value for money	• Receive relevant, clear, accurate and timely budget information and advice
	• An appropriate level of training and development prior to assuming financial responsibility

Figure 6.2 Responsibilities and rights

ACTIVITY **6.1**

In respect of your service area identify the budget manager.

i) Establish whether they have devolved, delegated, or pseudo-devolved responsibility.

ii) Identify their formal responsibilities with regard to budget management.

iii) Establish or propose a set of rights appropriate to their responsibilities.

iv) Reach a view as to whether their rights are observed by the organisation.

Financial competencies – managers

The breadth of financial competence needed by managers depends on the approach to finance within the organisation, their managerial level, whether budget responsibility is devolved or delegated and the level of support received from accountants and administrative staff.

Depending on their responsibilities managers should be able to:

- prepare a budget;
- monitor a budget;
- prepare year-end forecasts taking effective action, including as necessary escalating budget issues within the organisation.

In addition they should understand the:

- role, responsibilities and rights associated with their post;
- financial regulations and procedures within which they are expected to work;
- budget-reporting process and budget reports;
- political and behavioural aspects of budgeting.

Budget managers should periodically review their competence in the light of anticipated changes in the external environment and their future responsibilities. This later point encourages a manager to start preparing for their next financial role, which will often be more strategic, broader and complex.

At a more strategic level effective management may involve the use of specialist financial techniques and require a deeper understanding of financial management. Reassuringly perhaps, senior managers do not need to train to become accountants; as their roles become more onerous the level of technical support received from finance specialists should increase. It is important however that the manager resists the temptation to transfer responsibility for finance to accounting staff and has a broad understanding of financial techniques, can participate in their use and sensitively interpret and act upon the outcomes.

Chapter 7
Budget preparation

Introduction

This chapter defines budget management, provides an overview of the main processes involved and details different ways in which budgets can be prepared.

Definitions

For the purpose of this text budget management is defined as:

The total process by which budgets are prepared, negotiated, monitored and acted upon.

An expenditure budget is defined as:

The estimated cost of acquiring the use of the physical resources needed to pursue the actions planned to achieve the objectives, and ultimately the mission of the organisation.

And an income budget is defined as:

The estimated fees, charges, grants or other funding associated with the provision of one or more services or activities.

Two aspects of the above definitions are important. Firstly, budgets reflect a chosen view of the future and it follows that to some extent they will probably be incorrect. Secondly, there is an assumed link between the budget and the plan.

Whilst budgets can be expressed in units of physical resources, e.g. staff hours, miles, etc., they are more commonly expressed in financial terms and fall into two main types: those concerned with day-to-day running expenses and income (revenue) and those concerned with the purchase of items broadly expected to last more than one year (capital).

Figure 7.1 illustrates how in practice planning and budgeting are often managed as two separate processes, with the attendant risk that these produce different and unreconciled views of the future.

A charitable view is that this poor linkage results from the difficulty that managers in the service sector have of identifying how much physical resource is required for a certain level and quality of service. An alternative view is that if the linkage is denied or unclear, senior managers, politicians and society are free to demand ever higher levels and standards of service whilst maintaining or reducing resources.

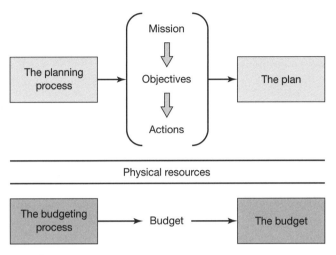

Figure 7.1 Separated processes

As argued previously, plans and budgets should be integrated, with both appearing as a single document or alternatively as two documents that dovetail. Figure 7.2 shows the integrated process in which physical resources clearly feature.

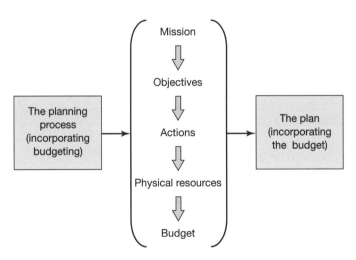

Figure 7.2 Integrated processes

By comparison, physical resources tend not to be taken into account in either the plan or budget, where separation is the practice.

Knowledge of the quantity and quality of physical resources needed to fulfil a plan and to calculate the budget is the key to integration. Budget management involves two major processes: preparation and control, as shown in Figure 7.3, which also shows that these link with activity management which incorporates planning.

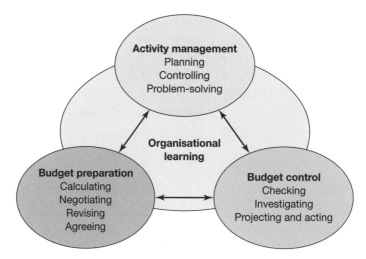

Figure 7.3 Budget management in context

Budget preparation involves calculating, negotiating, revising and agreeing the budget. Budgetary control involves checking, investigating, projecting and acting. The two processes of preparation and control should be managed so as to maximise learning; sound preparation should lead to learning that will assist with future budgetary control and control should lead to learning that will help when preparing the next budget.

An effective approach to budget management will:

● stimulate and improve service planning, co-ordination and control across the organisation;

● help ensure that plans are honest and realistic given the level of available resource, thereby minimising the risk that quality will be eroded;

● encourage the discussion of service priorities.

Unfortunately the practice of budget management is often poor and organisations fail to realise these potential benefits.

The budget cycle

Organisations tend to engage in similar patterns of budget management activity during the year, due in part to many of them working to the same financial year, which runs from April to March. However, the precise timings of the stages involved vary to reflect the size, complexity and approach to budget management.

In larger organisations the budget cycle for a particular year spreads over approximately two years, starting nine or more months before the year in question and concluding approximately three months after, as indicated in Figure 7.4.

Figure 7.4 A typical budget cycle

Budget and planning cycles should be similar and certainly link, the process for which should start with high-level discussions regarding the likely future environment as informed by the SPELT analysis. This will include factors such as anticipated pay settlements, inflation rates, interest rates, government grants, financial implications of new legislation, etc. The information derived from SPELT allows those planning to reach an initial view of 'how next year might look' in terms of likely overall resource levels and budget pressures. Once this future view is known, detailed plan and budget preparation commences and a cycle of preparation, negotiation and revision is repeated several times as grant settlements, likely inflation, etc., become clearer, closer to the start of the budget year. Budgets and service plans often therefore need to be fine-tuned prior to formal corporate agreement or approval.

Final plan and budget approval occurs almost immediately before the budget year starts and the manager's attention turns to performance monitoring, including budgetary control. Budgetary control is normally undertaken on a monthly basis and involves assessing and responding to the financial position to date and as anticipated for the year end.

Towards the end of the budget year and continuing into the early part of next year, attention shifts to closing the accounts, a process that ensures all income and expenditure relating to the budget year is identified and coded to the correct budgets. Closure, which is largely a technical exercise, tends to involve finance staff and administrators more than managers and results in the preparation of the final set of accounts.

In recent years two changes to the traditional budget cycle have occurred. Firstly, local authorities have been required to close accounts more quickly so the whole cycle ends earlier than it used to. Secondly, the preparation process tends to start earlier due to continued pressure on resources and greater complexity associated with increased partnership working. In some organisations the planning process is now continual with regular environmental scanning and modelling of financial impact, particularly at a corporate level.

Multi-agency working, which frequently involves resource sharing, means those planning need to time the multi-agency planning and budget preparation process so that it fits the cycles of different agencies. Failure to co-ordinate can leave a multi-agency team submitting a resource request for next year that is too late to be considered in the current round of agency plans and budgets.

Budget preparation

When preparing budgets one important aim is to ensure that planned activity can be resourced. As managers are rarely happy to reduce the quantity or quality of services they manage, there is a risk that they may accept or even propose a budget that is insufficient for planned activity, preferring to hope it will all 'work out' rather than confront the potential need for service reductions. Whilst occasionally luck or improvements in operation enable a plan to be achieved with fewer resources than originally estimated, it is more likely that a failure to confront budget problems will lead to:

- overspent budgets at the year end;

- lower than planned volumes of service, which allows the manager to keep within budget but will probably result in higher than budgeted unit costs;

- a fall in the quality of the service which will probably be noticed by service users but not necessarily acknowledged within the organisation;

- action that will have a negative long-term impact, for example failing to adequately maintain buildings or to develop staff;

- further increased pressure on staff which, in the longer term, may have cost implications.

There is a need for senior managers, political leaders and society to own the relationship between planned service provision, resource consumption and cost. If there is a wish to devote less money to a particular service the outcome of this needs to be recognised and owned at all organisational levels – pretending that the level of quantity and quality of service can be forever maintained whilst the level of resource is reduced year on year is unsustainable.

The first stage involved in budget preparation is calculation, this usually involving finance staff preparing an initial version of the budget based on the existing budget adjusted, or not, for the effects of inflation and other cost pressures between the two years. In those organisations that fail to engage devolved budget managers in budget preparation or where these managers lack competence or confidence, there is a danger that this initial version of the budget will be accepted, perhaps in the belief that as it was prepared by an accountant, it will be reliable. It is essential that devolved budget managers check any budget figures given to them to see if these look reasonable, either by independently calculating the resources they think they need or, at least, by reference to their experience of budget under- or overspends. Whilst arguably delegated managers do not need to be engaged in preparation it is still good practice for them to be consulted as it builds their understanding of the assumptions underpinning the budget and helps prepare them for more onerous responsibilities later in their career.

Budgets are financial targets and should be challenging yet realistic; qualities achieved through rigorous negotiation between the budget manager, their line manager and ultimately politicians, trustees, etc. To be effective in negotiation the budget manager needs knowledge of the service, planned activity and the relationship this has with physical resources.

Either the plan and/or the budget may need revision as a result of negotiation, this concluding with agreement as to the level of funding which should now be sufficient to resource the planned service.

Tips for success

In order to be successful in budget preparation:

- *managers should be properly engaged and able to reach a view as to the adequacy of the budget;*

- *sufficient time should be allocated to the budget process;*

- *there needs to be integration with the planning process and sufficient time allowed for detailed work and coordination;*

- *managers should have an opportunity to negotiate;*

- *the negotiation stage should be challenging;*

- *any decision to reduce or cap a budget should be accompanied by those involved owning the resultant implications for the service and adjusting planned activity accordingly;*

- *discussion with a line manager should take place, where appropriate, leading to budget revision and clear notification of the approved budget.*

As a consequence of poor preparation, budget managers are often unsure of the basis upon which the budget is prepared and unaware of whether the amount is adequate. This can lead to any of the following.

- A lack of commitment to stay within the approved budget amount.

- Stress and fear.

- Managers being unduly prudent and restricting spending early in the year to be on the 'safe side'. The resultant underspending, which may have been gained as a result of restricting service provision, is then corrected with a year-end 'spend up' which often represents poor value for money.

- Poor behaviour, game-playing and low morale.

Budget calculating

There are two broad approaches to preparing a budget: rational and historic. Rational approaches attempt to relate financial budgets to physical resource requirements, which in turn reflect the volume and quality of planned service. Rational approaches include policy-based budgeting, thematic, plan-led, needs-led, zero-based, etc.

Whilst a case can be made for rational budgeting this is a time-consuming process that is likely to yield little benefit if done each year, particularly in respect of services that are relatively stable.

With historic, or incremental budgeting as it is often known, a future budget is based on previous actual figures or more likely the existing budget.

In practice most organisations use a mixture of rational and historic techniques, skewed towards the historic. Whilst rational budgeting may be used for new services or as part of a fundamental review, historic budgeting will tend to be used elsewhere. Most organisations would benefit from increasing the proportion of budgets prepared on a rational basis, adopting a rolling programme whereby all budgets are completed on this basis one year in three with an historic approach used for the other two years.

Irrespective of whether a rational or historic approach is adopted, all budgets comprise two elements:

- the volume of physical resource to be purchased (e.g. the number of staff to be employed);

- the price (e.g. annual salary plus employer's national insurance and pension contributions).

These two elements are evident where rational budgeting is used but the process of historic budgeting obscures this, particularly where this simply involves adding an inflation factor to a previous budget figure.

Rational budgeting

The financial calculations associated with rational approaches to budget preparation are typically straightforward. However, estimating the quantity of physical resources required, on which the financial budget is based, can be difficult and requires considerable professional and service knowledge.

There are a number of different forms of rational budgeting including plan-led and zero-based, both of which are outlined below.

Plan-led

The case for integrating the planning and budgeting processes has been made earlier, the link between these being an estimate of the volume of physical resources required to support the plan.

As the most important factor in budget preparation within voluntary and public-sector organisations is usually the overall level of available resource, it is sensible to get an early indicator of the overall budget situation. This indication, which allows those planning and budgeting to be realistic about their aspirations and therefore their plans, should result from a high-level environmental scan and be communicated as general planning information or issued as a planning given.

Zero-based

In mature organisations it is common to find budgets that have been prepared on an historic basis for many years. The link between the plan and budget is vague at best; the budget is unlikely to have been challenged for some time and may be too generous, insufficient or even unnecessary.

Zero-based budgeting involves calculating the budget by reference to what is needed rather than previous or existing budget levels. Maximum benefit is derived when long-held assumptions about the need for, quality of and means of delivering the service are challenged. Potentially zero-based budgeting is a creative process involving deep consideration of what is to be done, how and to what standard. If undertaken well the manager will find the analysis focuses on service activity much more than financial costs and benefits, to the extent that it might be better referred to as zero-based planning.

Those involved in zero-based budgeting should be prepared to:

- challenge commonly held views regarding clients and their needs, the service and professional practice;

- develop a deep understanding of service outcomes and how these might be achieved;

- innovate in terms of service design and delivery.

It should be noted that writers often talk of this process involving 'justification', which is correct in the sense that whatever comes out of the process can be justified. However, in using this term there is a risk of implying that the aim is to justify what exists rather than challenging the *status quo*; the former being a natural temptation for managers and perhaps reinforced where zero-based budgeting is inappropriately talked of as a cost-cutting tool, which severely limits its effectiveness. Stakeholders, anxious to protect budgets, are likely to adopt change-resistant postures based on justifying why this budget can not be reduced rather than considering the value of the service, whether it should continue, and how. If undertaken thoroughly, zero-based budgeting will on occasion lead to a case being made for a larger rather than smaller budget, much in the same way as with effective best-value studies. Figure 7.5 identifies some of the reasons why lower and higher budgets may arise with zero-based budgeting.

Lower budgets may arise due to:	Higher budgets may arise due to:
Improved purchasing arrangements leading to economy gains	A need to correct problems arising from years of pushing costs into future years
More efficient use of resources resulting in less volume needing to be purchased	The process revealing practices or standards that are illegal or unacceptable – additional resources may be required to remedy this situation
Changing delivery processes which may affect the type, volume and mix of resources required. Overall the value of the resources required may fall	Recognising that a service which might be economic and efficient is not actually meeting the needs of clients and therefore of low value – additional resources are required
A reduction in planned service volumes – therefore less resource required	An increase in planned service volume or quality – therefore more physical resources required

Figure 7.5 Reasons for lower and higher budgets arising from zero-based budgeting

Challenging questions are at the heart of zero-based budgeting, the phrasing of which reflects the budget under review. Example questions such as those included in Figure 7.6 indicate the level of challenge applicable to a budget for travel associated with visiting clients in their own homes in order to undertake an assessment. The questions in this example form an early stage in preparing a zero-based budget, after which an estimate can be made of how many miles will need to be travelled which, when multiplied by the appropriate mileage rate, will lead to a financial budget. Typical of the early stages of zero-based budgeting, the answers to almost all the above questions involve knowledge of care, standards, professional practice, managerial factors, etc. In this example even more radical questions may be possible going beyond issues associated purely with travel and assessment.

1. What is the reason for visiting the client?

2. Are assessments necessary?

3. Why is it necessary to visit the client in their own home as at present?

4. Why not require the client to visit us or to use the telephone?

5. How often should each client be visited?

6. Could the assessment be undertaken as part of any other visit?

If a visit to the client at home is necessary

7. By what means should staff travel?

If for example, cars are deemed necessary

8. How might journeys be planned in the most travel efficient way?

9. Which is the most cost-effective way of organising car travel (e.g. pool cars, company cars, use of private cars)?

If private cars are to be used

10. What is the most appropriate rate to reimburse at?

Figure 7.6 Example zero-based budgeting questions

The advantages and limitations of rational budgeting approaches vary with the actual approach used. Figure 7.7 shows these in respect of zero based budgeting.

Zero-based budgeting	
Advantages are that it...	**Limitations are that it...**
Involves challenging the current service	Is time-consuming and can become unworkable
Is potentially creative	Requires an ability and willingness to challenge at all organisational levels
Engages managers and service professionals in budgeting	Places additional demands on finance staff
Is likely to ensure recognition of the service user viewpoint	Demands considerable non-financial information
Is a source of organisational learning and demonstrates a commitment to value for money	Can lead to an outcome that may conflict with the preferences of key stakeholders

Figure 7.7 Zero-based budgeting – advantages and limitations

It should be noted that many of the limitations associated with zero-based budgeting are reduced if this is undertaken as a rolling programme where a few budgets are subjected to this approach each year.

Historic budgeting

With historic, or incremental budgeting as it is often known, the budget for next year is based on previous actual expenditure or more frequently the budget relating to the current year.

In practice there are two forms of historic budgeting: full and partial. With the former version a fair attempt is made to ensure that the budget for next year adequately takes account of all financial implications of known or anticipated changes in the environment, the service offered or the price of resources required. Figure 7.8 is an example of how full incremental budgeting might look in respect of an establishment.

Establishment A	£
Budget for 2007/08 (current year)	1,450,000
Anticipated service changes (2008/09)	
Reduction in expected occupancy	-30,000
New quality standards	40,000
Implementation of new pay structure	20,000
Staff restructuring	-25,000
	1,455,000
Inflation (estimated at 3%)	44,000
Budget for 2008/09	**£1,499,000**

Figure 7.8 Historic budgeting example

In the above example the budgeted figure for 2008/09 (£1,499,000) should be sufficient providing that:

- the current budget for 2007/08 (£1,450,000) adequately reflects planned activity for 2007/08;

- all changes to service provision and operation in 2008/09 have been anticipated and the estimated financial implications are reasonably accurate.

The advantages and limitations associated with historic budgeting are summarised in Figure 7.9.

Historic budgeting	
Advantages are that it...	**Limitations are that it...**
Is easy to undertake and relatively inexpensive particularly in centralised organisations	Encourages the separation of planning and budgeting, thereby breaking the link between activity and resources
Is relatively quick to complete so budget preparation can start later in the year	Encourages the perpetuation of existing services and ways of operating
Results in relatively stable patterns of funding and service provision which assists central control	Does not normally lead to any slack in the budget being identified
Is less likely to result in resource rivalry due to increases or decreases tending to be applied incrementally and experienced to a similar extent by different services	Causes budget preparation to become a technical financial process from which many managers withdraw, leading to disempowerment

Figure 7.9 Historic budgeting – advantages and limitations

Incremental budgeting is widely practised in a 'partial' form where changes to the budget are made only for a limited range of reasons, for example inflation. This partial and rather crude approach has developed due to:

- a general unwillingness to confront the resource implications associated with increasing demand for service and improved quality;

- constant pressure to limit public spending;

- a belief that efficiency can be encouraged by setting budgets that are lower than required;

- limited understanding of the link between plans and budgets with consequently little way of knowing if existing budgets are too tight or generous.

Price bases

Irrespective of whether the chosen approach to budgeting is rational or historic, those leading organisations have to decide how to respond to inflation or changing prices. Figure 7.10 illustrates how inflation can impact on a budget.

Taking as an example a budget prepared in November for printer cartridges, to be purchased in the financial year starting next April.

Assuming it is expected that 100 printer cartridges will be needed next year and that at the date the budget is prepared these cost £20 each. Based on this price the budget needed next year will be £2,000 (100 times £20). This budget will prove sufficient if the planned volume (100 cartridges) is purchased and the price applying throughout next year remains at £20. However, if the price were to rise to £21 from 1 April and remain at this level for the whole year, the cost of 100 cartridges would be £2,100, which exceeds the original budget. Assuming the manager decides to keep within the budget by reducing the number of cartridges, only 95 can be purchased (£2000/21).

Figure 7.10 The impact of inflation

As budgets are prepared prior to the year to which they relate, the actual price that will be paid for resources is unknown. By the time resources are purchased the price may well be different, usually higher.

Inflation can be a significant problem, particularly when the rate is high and/or volatile; the risk being that the money available in the year will be insufficient to purchase the level of goods and services required to deliver the plan.

Leaders of organisations have two main options for dealing with inflation.

● Option A – Use the price that applied at the date budget preparation takes place. Many years ago this was a common way of pricing a budget and it works providing the budget manager is given additional money during the year if actual prices rise. However, whilst this approach protects the service provider from inflation it causes problems for those funding as they can not entirely predict how much they will have to give to the service provider.

● Option B – Base the price on what it is expected to pay during the year to which the budget relates, by incorporating an allowance for future inflation. Normally with this basis, once the budget is agreed it remains fixed during the year irrespective of whether the amount of inflation was estimated correctly. This approach works well for budget managers providing that future inflation is estimated correctly and is helpful to service funders who will know with certainty and in advance how much they will pay for a service to be delivered.

Returning to the last example, the following figures compare the two approaches to inflation.

If the organisation adopts the approach described as Option A, those funding the service will be asked to top up the £2,000 by £100 to £2,100 (100 times £1).

If Option B is adopted with the budget based on expected price levels an allowance will be built into the budget to cover anticipated future rises in price. If the person preparing the budget has perfect foresight they will estimate that the effect of future inflation will be 5% and the budget, would be £2,100 (£2,000 plus 5%). As few people can forecast inflation perfectly, the approved budget will normally prove to be too low or high depending on the estimated and actual rates of inflation. If for example at the point at which the budget was set the expected effect of inflation next year was 3%, the budget would have been as follows

Budget	*£*
At current prices (100 cartridges at £20)	*2,000*
Anticipated effect of inflation (3% on £2,000)	*60*
Total budget	*2,060*
Actual expenditure (100 at £21)	*2,100*
Potential overspend	*40*

If no managerial action is taken, the budget will be overspent by £40 by the year end. Alternatively, if the budget manager tries to keep within budget only 98 cartridges (98 x £21=£2,058) will be purchased, resulting in an underspend of £2 (£2,060 less £2,058).

Tips for success

As a budget holder make sure you understand how inflation is treated in your organisation, the implications this has for your budget and how you may need to manage during the year.

- *If the prices prevailing when the budget was prepared (Option A) are used you should find out the process by which additional budget can be secured to cover inflation.*

- *If future prices are used (Option B) you should find out the rate of inflation that was used and reach a view as to the adequacy of this provision. Be prepared to challenge the rate(s) of inflation used and monitor the prices actually incurred during the year.*

Employee budgets

For many managers in social care and health their largest budget relates to employee costs; in practice often being so large that if not managed properly it will inevitably have a significant effect on the overall budget position.

Whilst incremental and zero-based approaches to budget preparation can be used with employee budgets there are three other common approaches: full-staff establishment, anticipated staff costs and mid-scale, as explained below.

Full-staff establishment

With this approach the employee budget is based on the staff structure, terms and conditions of employment expected to apply during the budget year, together with the grade and spinal column points relating to current post-holders. For each existing post-holder an estimate is made of the salary they will receive next year as appropriate, including increments, performance-related pay, annual pay award, etc. If there are any anticipated changes to the structure, terms and conditions these will be incorporated, as will currently vacant posts at appropriate rates.

This approach should lead to a budget that will be sufficient to meet the cost of employing staff next year. In practice this often leads to an underspend due to members of staff leaving and not being replaced for some time.

It should be noted that this approach should not be confused with zero-based budgeting as no attempt is made to challenge the current staff establishment, skill mix, remuneration package, etc.

Anticipated staff costs

Where staff budgets are underspent due to staff turnover, this can be embarrassing as the money saved could have been used for additional service provision. A common way of trying to avoid this problem is to deduct from the full-staff establishment budget as described above, an amount equal to the savings expected to arise from staff turnover.

There are a number of drawbacks with this approach.

- The budget manager starts the year with a budget that will be insufficient to meet their staff costs should they experience zero staff turnover.

- Estimating the impact of future staff turnover is difficult as it is affected by role, age, gender, seniority, economic environment, etc.

- Where staff budgets are devolved the number of staff within a cost centre may be relatively few, which means that the actual experience of turnover is likely to vary significantly from one cost centre to another and from one year to the next.

- In practice some staff vacancies may have to be covered through overtime or the use of agency staff, the cost of which may well be greater than the savings released. For a few services there is a case to be made for adding a factor for turnover rather than deducting it.

Mid-scale

Another approach to calculating employee budgets, which is attractive because it is simple and easy to use, is 'mid-scale'. Irrespective of the spinal column points on which actual staff will be paid, the budget is based on the midpoint of the scale. Figure 7.11 below illustrates the impact of using the mid-scale approach for a cost centre employing ten full-time staff on a grade that starts at £15,000 and rises in five equal increments to £19,000.

Scale Point	Salary	Midpoint	Number of staff	Budget
5	£19,000			
4	£18,000			
3	£17,000	£17,000	10	£170,000
2	£16,000			
1	£15,000			

In a financial 'worst case' scenario, all staff would be on the top of the scale and expected expenditure therefore £190,000, whilst the budget is based on £170,000. In the event that there is no staff turnover the budget will be £20,000 overspent at the end of the year.

Figure 7.11 Mid-scale salary – example

In practice the budget is normally set too low to meet the cost of staff in post, unless there is sufficient turnover to provide offsetting savings. Occasionally however, the budget will be too generous, for example where the service is new or there has been significant turnover in recent years with new staff recruited on low incremental points.

Issues for budget managers

Different ways of calculating employee budgets leave the manager with different potential gaps between the budget and the total amount they may need to pay their staff next year. As a budget manager it is important to understand how the budget has been prepared, the assumptions made and the size of any potential gap between the budget and likely spending on staff.

Another potential issue for the manager is whether they have financially responsibility for any other employee-related costs that may or may not be allowed for in their agreed budget; for example, costs associated with long-term sickness and maternity. These can be difficult to predict, volatile over time and significant in size.

Tips for success
If you have responsibility for a staff budget you should do the following.

1. *Calculate how much you think your staff will cost next year, assuming no staff turnover.*

2. *Identify the organisational approach to estimating employee budgets and establish the resultant budget figure.*

3. *Calculate the difference between (1) and (2) above, identifying whether a potential under- or overspend is likely.*

4. *Consistent with good budget practice, alert your line manager to any potential under- or overspend as early as possible.*

5. *Plan how to manage any under- or overspend. In most cases there is likely to be a potential overspend which without employee turnover, will be very difficult to meet. However, it is the responsibility of the budget manager to take reasonable steps to offset any overspends through action related to other expenditure or income budgets.*

In addition you should establish the following.

6. *Whether budget responsibility for staffing includes meeting the financial consequences of long-term sickness or maternity cover and whether this is allowed for in your budget.*

7. *Whether the budget includes a reasonable allowance for the expected effect of future pay awards.*

8. *What will happen if the annual pay award is settled at a rate different to that assumed in the budget.*

Chapter 8
Budgetary control

Introduction

This chapter explains the budgetary control process, introduces the reader to profiling and commitment recording, explains how to read a budget report, undertake budgetary control and prepare a year-end forecast.

Budgetary control

Budgetary control is the process by which managers check and respond to the evolving position on actual income and expenditure budgets during the year. At its simplest the process involves:

- checking that financial information is accurate;

- comparing actual income and expenditure figures with what was expected up to this point in the year, identifying and investigating any significant differences, or variances;

- projecting the likely budget position at the year end and taking action as required.

Budgetary control should not be a stand-alone process; rather it should be an integral part of performance management. Effective budgetary control has the following properties.

- It causes budget managers to engage with, and act upon, financial information.

- It permits the early identification of potential underspends in a way that enables action resulting in the best use of resources, rather than perhaps a year-end 'spend up'.

- It permits the early identification of potential overspends, this allowing gentle corrective action rather than the more brutal action needed when overspending budgets become apparent towards the year end. Early action reduces the likelihood that clients fail to receive the standard of service they need, avoids staff being put under intense and unnecessary pressure and helps preserve performance and morale.

- It reduces the likelihood of 'stop/go' purchasing and the consequential negative impact on clients, staff and other stakeholders.

- It is a source of organisational learning.

Reporting process

The process of reporting and acting on budget variance varies between organisations, according to whether responsibility for budgetary control is assumed by:

• Finance staff who can actually only go so far before having to ask the budget manager for help to understand important variances and take action. In this type of organisation it is common to find senior managers and politicians turning to accountants for budget information rather than their budget managers. There is an associated risk that the manager believes that the accountant is 'looking after the money' and therefore engages even less in the financial aspects of their role; a vicious circle is created.

• Managers are assisted by finance staff who provide financial information and technical support, along with corporate-level strategic budget monitoring. Budget estimation, negotiation, approval and control are all exercised within the managerial line.

Three key questions

Three key questions typically provide the focus for budgetary control:

• How are we doing?

• How much of the budget is left?

• What will the year-end position look like?

Whilst a few managers will consider all these questions, more will typically focus on only one or perhaps two of these, according to organisational practice and/or, personal preference.

1. How are we doing?

This question focuses entirely on what has happened so far in the current budget year. Figure 8.1 provides budget information for the first five months of the year in respect of stationery. The budget for the whole year is £12,000 and expenditure is expected to be even throughout the year.

Budget for £12,000	Budget to 31 August	Actual to 31 August	Variance to 31 August
	(£)	(£)	(£)
Stationery	5,000	4,912	-88

Figure 8.1 Budgetary control example 1

At this point in the year the budget is underspent by £88.

In this example an underspend is shown as negative whereas an overspend would be positive. With regard to how underspends and overspends are shown on budget reports there is little consistency between, and sometimes even within, organisations. Plusses, minuses, brackets and colours are all used and the manager should always check they understand the approach to presenting underspends and overspends prior to reading a financial report.

Figure 8.1 shows the cumulative position, that is, all expenditure up to and including that occurring in Month 5. In some organisations this will be accompanied by the same information but relating to the last month, as shown in Figure 8.2, which shows that £80 of the £88 underspending occurred in August.

Budget for the year £12,000	Budget for August	Actual for August	Variance for August	Budget for year to 31 Aug	Actual for year to 31 Aug	Variance for year to 31 Aug
	(£)	(£)	(£)	(£)	(£)	(£)
Stationery	1,000	920	-80	5,000	4,912	-88

Figure 8.2 Budgetary control – example 2

2. How much of the budget is left?

Knowing how much budget is left to spend at a point in the year is important information, calculated by deducting actual expenditure to date from the budget for the whole year. Returning to the earlier example, it appears that £7,088 (£12,000 – £4,912) is left to be spent.

3. What will the year-end position look like?

Ultimately budget performance tends to be judged on whether the manager has kept within the budget for the whole year. Overspends and underspends at various points in the year tend to be forgotten if at the year end spending is within budget and income equal to or in excess of that budgeted.

Increasingly the practice within organisations is to make regular estimates of the final year-end position. These figures are known variously as estimated out-turn, projected out-turn, forecast year-end and budget-holder forecast.

In practice there are two main ways of estimating the year end.

- Reference to the actual income and expenditure at the current point in the year. So if stationery expenditure at Month 5 is £4,912 the year-end prediction figure would be £11,788, arrived at by dividing the actual to date by the number of months it relates to and multiplying by 12.

$$\frac{\text{Actual to date}}{\text{Months to date}} \times 12 \qquad \frac{£4,912}{5} \times 12 \quad = £11,788$$

For those budgets where the same amount of money will be spent each month this approach is fine. However, for many budgets the rate of spend varies during the year and predictions calculated this way can be seriously flawed. Returning to the stationery example for which there is a total budget for the year of £12,000 – if instead of spending approximately the same amount each month the practice is to bulk-purchase £5,000 of stationery by the end of April, the predicted out-turn at month 1 using this basis would be £60,000 (£5,000/1*12).

- Combining the actual to date with an estimate of expenditure or income for the rest of the year. As this calculation is best done by the budget manager this should really be referred to as a budget manager forecast. This figure should take account of spend to date, reasons for any variance to date plus anticipated spend for the rest of the year.

Profiling

One key piece of information needed for budgetary control purposes is the amount of the budget that it is expected to be spent or earned by a particular point in time, often referred to in budget statements as 'budget to date', or budget profile.

In effect the annual budget comprises 12 monthly budgets, the relative size of each determined by factors such as service activity, weather, contracts of employment, etc. Good-quality profiling is essential to good budgetary control; however, it is still quite common to find budget statements where the profile is simply assumed to be 'even' each month. This practice can be very misleading, as shown in Figure 8.3, which concerns a stationery budget where the practice is to bulk-buy in April and September, each time spending 50% of the budget. Actual spending is shown in dark grey and the budget profile in light grey.

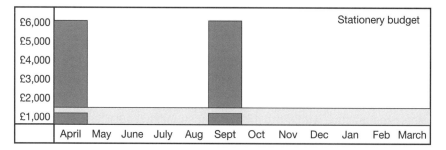

Figure 8.3 Profile and actual comparison (based on incorrect 'even' profile)

Based on these figures a budgetary control statement would incorrectly show an overspend for most of the year – at the end of April the overspend would be £5,000 (£1,000 profiled budget less £6,000 of actual spending). This overspend would reduce each month to September when it would increase to £6,000 (£12,000 of total spending less £6,000 of profiled budget). From October onwards the overspend would decrease each month and assuming that no more expenditure occurs during the year the total spending at the year end would be identical to the original budget. All the overspend figures for the first 11 months are incorrect due to inappropriate profiling and could cause the reader to misunderstand the budget position and take inappropriate control action.

Commitments

Main accounting systems vary in terms of the point at which a transaction is recorded and becomes formally 'known' in the organisation.

In many public-sector organisations income appears on the main accounting system at the earliest opportunity with cash, cheques, etc., appearing when they are banked and invoice income as soon as invoices are issued. Income figures therefore tend to be reasonably up to date, something which is rarely true of expenditure figures due to the widespread practice of recognising expenditure only when payments are made rather than when orders are issued. As a consequence there will be instances of orders raised in respect of which invoices have yet to be received and expenditure is therefore understated.

As it is important to have up-to-date income and expenditure information during the year, managers in many organisations manually combine payment information from the main system with local information regarding outstanding orders, etc.

Commitment recording systems record information in respect of orders raised, deliveries received, and invoices passed for payment. At present many commitment systems are manual or involve the use of spreadsheets. This is likely to change as newer accounting systems are acquired that have a capacity to incorporate online order processing and hold commitment information. When designing local commitment systems it is wise to ask finance staff for advice regarding the format as there are many different formats, one of which might be better suited to your service. Of crucial importance is to ensure that budget to date information (profile) and commitment information are prepared on a comparable basis and that those using this understand any assumptions made.

Figure 8.4 illustrates the potential impact of including commitments in budgetary control information.

This example relates to a budget of £100,000 of which £80,000 is expected (profiled) to have been spent by the end of month eight.

Payments of £73,500 appear on the computer and at first glance therefore it appears that this budget is underspent by £6,500 (£80,000 – £73,500) and £26,500 (£100,000 – £73,500) remains in the budget. However, assuming in this example that the total value of official orders issued but not yet paid is £7,500, the position is actually quite different. In order to get a more realistic view of actual spending and what is left, the value of outstanding orders needs to be taken into account.

Figure 8.4 Impact of commitments on budget information

	£	£
Budget for year		*100,000*
	£	£
Profiled budget (months 1–8)		*80,000*
Payments (months 1–8)	*73,500*	
Commitments (months 1–8)	*7,500*	
Expenditure (months 1–8)		*81,000*
Budget position (overspent at month 8)		*1,000*
Budget remaining		*19,000*

Figure 8.4 continued

When operating a commitment system it is essential to ensure regular reconciliation with the actual expenditure recorded on the main accounting system.

Understanding budget reports

Whilst budget report formats vary from one organisation to the next, and even within an organisation, the extent of this variation tends to be fairly limited; being more to do with the order in which information is provided and terminology used, both of which reflect the traditions of the organisation and preferences of finance staff. Figure 8.5 is an extract from a typical budget report, together with an explanation as to the content.

When reading a budget statement the budget manager should ensure they understand:

- how the annual budget (column 3) was prepared, the plan it links to and whether it includes an allowance for inflation;

- how the budget has been profiled (column 4) and be assured that this is realistic;

- how up to date the actual figure (column 5) is and be prepared to add to this any expenditure that is committed but has not yet been taken into account;

- how underspends and overspends are shown on the system and be clear as to what constitutes a significant variance (columns 6 and 7);

- the accuracy of the budget unspent figure and how this will need to change if any commitments have to be taken into account;

- what is expected of them regarding the budget manager forecast and be able to prepare appropriate figures.

Forecasting the year end

Of increasing importance to understanding the budget position is the ability of the budget manager to estimate year-end figures.

Where organisations devolve budget responsibility, effective control is dependent on managers more than accountants and there is an opportunity to move away from pro-rata end-of-year calculations and adopt budget manager estimates.

Good-quality estimates of the likely year-end budget position combine:

- accurate actual income and expenditure information in respect of the year to date;

- anticipated expenditure for the rest of the year taking account of the estimated financial impact of changes in the service and intended actions in respect of any underspend and overspends to date.

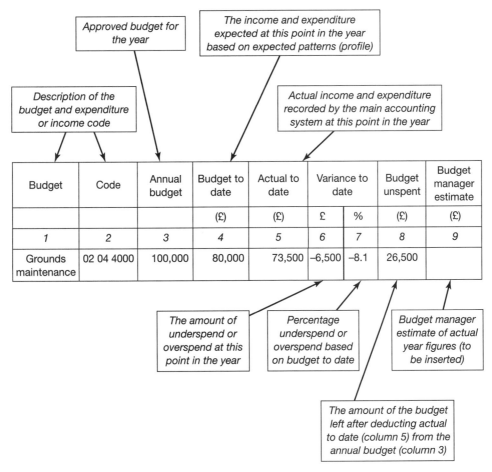

Figure 8.5 Example budget report

Control action

Effective budgetary control requires good-quality information, careful consideration of variances, honest estimates of the year-end position and early action.

Control action which is normally triggered in response to significant variances can take many forms, including for example:

- taking steps to increase or decrease service volume and quality over the remaining months of the year to bring the need for resources in line with remaining budget;

- reminding staff of the need to plan and control their use of resources carefully;

- delaying committing particular expenditure for the time being or even perhaps for the rest of the year;

- moving money between budgets, a practice common in some voluntary and most public-sector organisations, and referred to as virement.

Understanding budgetary control

When undertaking budgetary control, care should be taken to avoid two risks: spending excessive time on the process and missing potentially significant variances. Small under-spends or overspends are inevitable on almost every budget and the effective budget manager will focus on those variances that, without action, might develop into something significant. This ability to spot potential problems requires knowledge of the service plan, experience of service operation and ultimately judgement.

Budgetary control should be undertaken on a monthly basis by the responsible manager and supported by administrative staff and accountants. The process can be seen as comprising three stages, all of which are important and the responsibility of the budget manager, although not necessarily undertaken by them personally. Figure 8.6 illustrates these three stages. Depending on the systems and processes that are in place, stage 1 could be undertaken by administrative staff, particularly if they also are responsible for maintaining commitment records. With appropriate guidance regarding how to identify significant variances these staff might also undertake stage 2.

Stage 3, however, should always be completed personally by the responsible budget manager as only they will have the appropriate knowledge and skills needed to complete the year-end forecast and the authority to take management action. The following example explains this process in detail.

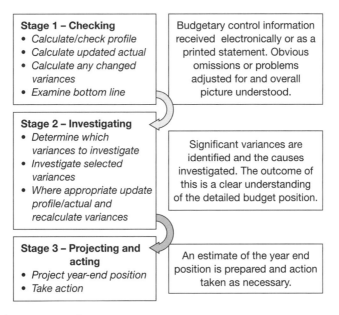

Figure 8.6 Budgetary control stages

Figure 8.7 is an example of budgetary control relating to a day centre for older people for which the manager is responsible for four budgets.

The annual budget includes an allowance for the effect of future inflation and the budget to dat is based on the amount that it is expected will be spent by this point in the year. Copier payments are monthly by direct debit. There is £500 of food which has been ordered, used and in respect of which the invoice has been passed for payment – however, this is not included in the actual to date. The printout covers the first six months of the financial year, April to September.

Budget	Annual budget (£)	Budget to date (£)	Actual to date (£)	Variance to date (£) (%)		Budget unspent (£)	Budget-holder forecast (£)
Copier rental	1,200	600	600	0	0	600	
Copier usage	600	250	299	49	20	301	
Gas	2,400	960	734	−226	−24	1,666	
Food	10,000	4,200	3,951	−249	−6	6,049	
Total	14,200	6,010	5,584	−426	−7	8,616	

Stage 1 – Checking
The first thing to note is that the overall budget expected to have been spent at this point in the year is £6,010 whilst actual expenditure is lower at £5,584 – an underspend at this point of £426 which on the face of it appears good news. There are perhaps no obvious problems with the profile behind the budget-to-date figures. A check of transactions reveals that the actual food expenditure is lower than it should be by £500 due to a commitment. If the invoice is included, actual food expenditure would be £4,451, resulting in an overspend of £251 for food and changing the overall surplus of £426 into a deficit of £74.

Figure 8.7 Budgetary control example

Stage 2 – Investigating

When deciding which variances to investigate a number of factors come into play, including the following.

i) Size of variance (expressed in pounds) – For many managers this is the most important criterion causing attention to be focused on large amounts of money. There is no golden rule as to what constitutes a large variance; this depends on a number of factors, particularly context.

ii) Size of variance (expressed as a percentage) – Percentages are a popular criterion, often associated with a threshold figure above which an investigation is triggered, e.g. 5%. This approach does pose one significant risk in that a large percentage variance on a small budget might trigger attention whilst a small percentage variance on a larger budget could go unnoticed, even though it might be of much higher monetary value.

iii) Knowledge of the service – A good budget manager who has been actively engaged in budget preparation will have a sense of which budgets are more volatile or sensitive and therefore need to be watched carefully.

It should be noted that underspends and overspends are of equal concern. Looking at each budget in turn for the purpose of this exercise, we note the following.

Copier rental is on track – the budget to date is based on a regular amount each month, which has been paid. There is no under/overspend and the amount left for the rest of the year looks adequate.

Copier usage – currently overspent by £49 (20%), there could be some problems at the year end if this continues. The sum involved is not great but it might be worth raising this at the next team meeting and monitoring this again next control period.

Gas – underspent by £226 (24%). This variance is quite large and raises questions as to the validity of the profile and whether the expected number of quarterly bills has been paid. If one bill is outstanding then the 'real actual' will be quite a bit higher, probably making this overspend rather than underspend.

Food – underspent by £249 (6%) but after adjusting for the commitment is actually overspent by £251 (6%). This is not a large overspend in terms of the amount or percentage involved but might need to be watched as this is a budget where control can be lost quite quickly. It would be worth mentioning this to the chef and looking at it again next month.

Of the four budgets it can be argued that only gas needs investigating; copier usage and food would be worth mentioning to staff and then monitoring.

The process of investigation involves looking at the detailed transactions that make up the recorded expenditure to check that these relate to the service involved, are complete and correct. A comparison can then be made with the budget profile in terms of what was expected, for example were two quarters of gas bills are included in the profile but only one has been paid. If the correct number of quarters has been paid, investigating the underspend might reveal a number of causes; for example, that:

i) the price paid for gas is lower than what was expected when the budget was set;

ii) the tariff has changed;

iii) less gas has been consumed than expected.

Stage 3 – Projecting and acting

At this point the budget manager should understand the overall budget position, be aware of any significant underspends or overspends and the causes. Two further steps need to be completed: estimating the year-end budget and taking action.

An estimate of the likely year-end budget position involves taking account of experience so far this year and estimating future service resource needs. The following format is one way of presenting a budget-holder forecast.

Budget	Annual budget	Actual months 1–6	Estimate months 7–12	Budget manager forecast	Variance for year
1	2	3	4	5	6
Gas	2,400	734	?	?	?

Figure 8.7 continued

Information for the first three columns is as shown in the latest budget report. Column 3 might need to be adjusted depending on the outcome of any variance investigations, for example if a gas bill had been coded elsewhere in the organisation. Column 4 is an estimate of the expenditure that will be needed for the rest of the year, reflecting a number of factors including anything learnt as a result of the investigation.

As an example, assume the investigation reveals that:

● as expected, two gas bills have been paid, are correctly coded and error-free;

● gas consumption is at the level expected;

● the underspend is entirely due to a significant reduction in gas prices that is predicted to continue for the foreseeable future.

The figure to be included in column 4 can be calculated in different ways, for example starting with the budget that was originally expected to be needed for the last six months of the year (£2,400 for the year less £960 for the first six months), which equals £1,440. As gas prices have fallen by 24% below what was expected, one view of the rest of the year is that it will cost £1,094 (£1,440 less 24%).

Column 5 is simply the result of adding £734 to £1,094, which equals £1,828. Column 6 is the variance for the whole year, this resulting from a comparison of the budget with the budget manager forecast.

Budget	Annual budget £	Actual months 1–6 £	Estimate months 7–12 £	Budget manager forecast £	Variance for year £
1	2	3	4	5	6
Gas	2,400	734	1,094	1,828	−572

With regard to this budget there is a reasonable predicted underspend. The manager may wish to leave this sum where it is for the moment or transfer part or all of it to another budget where it can be used to fund an overspending situation or even boost spending in an area where there is an identified service need.

This is of course only one view of the future based on an assumption that prices remain lower than budgeted. A different and more prudent view would be that prices return to budgeted levels for the rest of the year, in which case the budget manager forecast would be £2,174 (£734 actual to date plus £1,440 which was the original budget for the rest of the year).

Figure 8.7 continued

A final note here is that a good budget manager will consider their budgets individually and on a collective basis. The answer to a problem on one budget, for example copier usage, may be to control another one, for example gas, more closely.

Conclusion

The intention behind writing this text was to promote effective planning and budget management and prompt the development of associated competence. The content provides a starting point for achieving this aim and with practice you should feel able to use the techniques included with competence and confidence. There is considerable scope for further personal development by extending your repertoire of planning techniques and knowledge of cost behaviour and analysis. The books referred to in the references are a good initial source of learning for anyone wishing to further develop their competence in planning and budget management.

References

Bean, J and Hussey, L (1996) *Managing the devolved budget*. London: HB Publications.

CIPFA (2001) *Financial Regulations: A good practice guide for an English Modern Council*. CIPFA Publications.

Drury, C (1994) *Costing: An introduction*. 3rd edition. London: Chapman Hall.

Johnson, G, Scholes, K and Whittington, R (2005) *Exploring corporate strategy*. Harlow: Pearson Education.

Luffman, G, Sanderson, S and Kenny, B (1987) *Business policy – An analytical introduction*. Oxford: Blackwell.

Mintzberg H, Ahlstrand, B and Lampel, J (1998) *Strategy safari*. Harlow: Prentice Hall.

Semple Piggot, C (2000) *Business planning for healthcare management*. Milton Keynes: Open University Press.

Index

Added to the page number 'f' denotes a figure.